Food
Markets of
the World

Food Markets of the World

Photographs by
Nelli Sheffer

Text by
Mimi Sheraton

Harry N. Abrams Inc., Publishers

Editor: Elisa Urbanelli

Designer: Carol Robson

To Udit—N.S.

Library of Congress Cataloging–in–Publication Data

Sheraton, Mimi.
      Food markets of the world / photographs by Nelli Sheffer ;
text by Mimi Sheraton.
          p.   cm.
     ISBN 0–8109–1184–1
     1. Cookery, International. 2. Farmers' markets. I. Title.
TX725.A1S442 1997
641.59—dc21   97–7953

"Western Star" by Stephen Vincent Benét
Holt, Rhinehart & Winston, Inc.
Copyright 1943 by Rosemary Carr Benét
Copyright renewed © 1971 by Rachel Benét Mahin,
Thomas C. Benét and Stephanie Benét Mahin
Reprinted by permission of Brandt & Brandt Literary
Agents, Inc.

Photographs copyright © 1997 Nelli Sheffer

Text copyright © 1997 Mimi Sheraton

Printed and bound in Hong Kong

Harry N. Abrams, Inc.
100 Fifth Avenue
New York, N.Y. 10011
www.abramsbooks.com

Page 1: *Tosardi, Java*
Title page: *Yogyakarta, Java*
Contents page: *Fuyang, Zhejiang Province, China*
Following pages, in sequence:
Zanzibar, Tanzania;
Tosardi, Java; Zanzibar, Tanzania;
Palermo, Italy; Munich, Germany;
Ubud, Bali; Denpasar, Bali;
Ho Chi Minh City (formerly Saigon), Vietnam; Beijing, China;
Nairobi, Kenya; Zanzibar, Tanzania;
Ipanema, Brazil; Chichicastenango, Guatemala;
Zanzibar, Tanzania; Chichicastenango, Guatemala

Contents

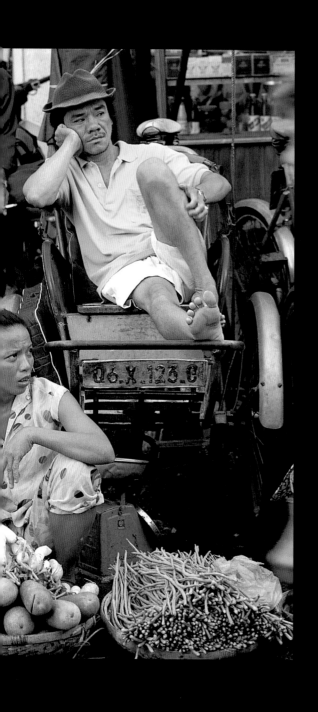

Introduction

M I M I   S H E R A T O N

And all along the road, and along the neighboring roads, in front and behind, the distant rumbling of vehicles told of the presence of similar contingents of the great caravan which was traveling onward through the gloom and deep slumber of that early hour, lulling the dark city to continued repose with its echoes of passing food.

—On produce being delivered to the old Les Halles market in Paris,
from *The Belly of Paris* by Emile Zola

Nelli Sheffer roams the world's food markets taking pictures with his camera. I roam those markets taking pictures in my mind. His glowing results are gathered here to entice all who care to look. Mine are more private, summoned into view by a sort of mental slide lantern, illuminating memories I hope will never dim.

My love affair with these opulent, lively markets began when I was a child. My father was in the wholesale fruit and produce business at the Washington Market in lower Manhattan, close to the Hudson River. When the family was out late for some celebration, say to dinner and the theater, he would look in on that market around midnight, taking us with him. As trucks rolled in from all over the country, porters unloaded burlap sacks of potatoes from Idaho; onions from Texas; crates of lemons, artichokes, and celery from California; bushel baskets of peaches from Georgia; and string beans from nearby farms in New Jersey and Pennsylvania. They placed them under big metal sheds hung onto lopsided narrow brick buildings, many of which had been the homes of early Dutch settlers in New Amsterdam.

It was a magical sight to a small child, the damp dark night lit by bare bulbs hanging under the sheds, bonfires in tall metal drums so workers could warm their hands, and the headlights of the trucks trained on the street to add brightness. Always there was the smell that I still recognize in vegetable markets the world over: a heady combination of the wet orange wood that formed crates, freshly rotted greens crushed underfoot on the damp sidewalk, the warm,

Brilliant tomatoes appear in midsummer at the Union Square Greenmarket in New York.

sweet overtones of onions and garlic, and an astringent citrus scent here and there. Intermittently, there were whiffs of strong hot coffee and even stronger whiskey, knocked back neat by workers who needed sustenance to see them through a night that would end at six the next morning. Then they would go into a corner tavern and down supper-breakfasts of Western omelets, London broil with mushroom gravy, steaks topped with fried eggs, and, in season, piles of fried soft-shell crabs.

What with so much eating and shouting as the all-male cast barked orders and clinched deals, they seemed highly privileged to me. They were awake and having what looked like a marvelous time while the rest of the city slept. Even now, I particularly cherish memories of night markets with the chiaroscuro magic of Xi'an in China, the snowy Christkindlmarkt in Munich, and, the old-time charmers, Les Halles in Paris and London's Covent Garden.

When we traveled to Los Angeles, the farmers' market, then true to its name, was my favorite sight, with free, freshly squeezed orange juice dispensed nonstop amid the stands of locally grown vegetables, all beautiful enough to be in a florist's shop. Among them was the strange alligator pear that we now call avocado. Later there was a trip to New Orleans and the romantically named French market, with its hanging ropes of braided garlic, its green satsumas and crimson Creole tomatoes, its pale jade mirliton squashes, and bushels of okra as delicate as pinky fingers. (In fact, the Arabic word for that luscious green pod is *bamia*, meaning "lady's finger.") It was exciting to see signs in French that I did not understand, and "cher," as in *chérie,* was the local term of address by vendors to any woman shopper. Then we ate at Morning Call, reviving ourselves with chicory-laced coffee soothed with hot milk and puffy, golden beignets, snowy with confectioners' sugar. With such early conditioning, it's no wonder I cannot resist a food market, anywhere, anytime.

By the time I got to Paris in 1953, I was primed for the legendary nocturnal delights of Les Halles, with its soaring glass-enclosed pavilions supported by graceful cast-iron columns. Part of Baron Haussmann's plan to redevelop Paris and begun in 1854 to designs by Victor Baltard and Félix Callet, this gorgeous market and the life of its merchant-inhabitants inspired the delicious novel *The Belly of Paris* (1873) by Emile Zola; in French or in English, it is a book no food or market lover should resist. With its game stalls and cheese stands; its exquisite vegetables and exotica such as snails, grassy sea urchins, and pale pink frogs' legs; its wild woodland strawberries, slim silky leeks, and lacy lettuces, Les Halles made one ready for a bowl of hot onion soup encrusted with melted cheese or a grilled pig's foot or two, veneered with garlicky, crunchy breadcrumbs.

Like many markets that catered mostly to a wholesale trade, Les Halles outgrew the city center, needing more space than was practical in a neighborhood with high real estate values, and more traffic arteries than possible there. (The Billingsgate fish market in London and the Washington Market in New York met the same fate.) Now, Paris's market is set in the more modern environs of Rungis, but I feel privileged to have known the old Les Halles. With its democratic mix of clientele that combined prostitutes and their *maquereaux,* swells in evening gowns and dinner jackets, artists wearing whatever, and wide-eyed tourists like me, it was, perhaps, the most stylishly urbane market the world has known.

The elements that made these markets irresistible exist in all markets. First, of course, there is the food itself, as beautiful and tempting to the gourmand, whose appetite is whetted in an atmosphere promising new or favorite old taste sensations, as to the artist, who appreciates form and color. Caillebotte, inspired by boxes of pears, apples, and plums, painted *Fruit,* giving it the subtitle *Display of Passion.* Taste and sight are not the only senses engaged at markets, for there are the scents and the sounds and the gentle touching of a soft-fuzzed peach or a cool, firm cabbage. And not too incidentally, at most markets there is the golden opportunity to eat—at snack stands, cafés, or full-fledged restaurants.

For the traveler, markets provide valuable insight into foreign cultures, affording one of the few windows on real life open to strangers. Very few markets are completely faked for tourists, some exceptions being portions of the floating market in Bangkok, sections of New Orleans's French market, and, one suspects, Holland's cheese market in Alkmaar, a three-hundred-year-old working institution where porters don antique costumes to do their jobs, and so create a favorite tourist sight.

More realistically, people buying and selling food mean business and, with mixed undertones of passion and planning, are intent on what they are doing. One feels this most in Paris, where many shop before lunch and dinner and so are fervid with hunger and anticipation, much more so than when shopping in a supermarket with a list of things to cook four days hence. Public manners, the socially correct and restrained demeanor displayed on the bus or on the street, may well fall away as a hurried mother decides what to feed the family for dinner, or a young man or woman chooses enticements to break down a lover's defenses. One also can observe if the people are polite to each other, how children talk to their parents, and if customers stand in orderly lines or push madly. And how does a merchant react when an especially annoying shopper presses his or her thumb into half-a-dozen pears, then buys none?

Most practically, markets give travelers a chance to see what foods they might want to try in restaurants, and there is often a chance to taste in situ. I always pack a knife, fork, and spoon in my luggage in case I am beguiled by a wayward slab of pâté, a wedge of nice runny cheese, or an especially plump eclair. Beyond the food itself, modes of display indicate the sophistication of public taste, which is particularly advanced in Japan and France, where the aesthetics of presentation are highly valued.

Markets can provide clues to the level of trust between citizens. How carefully do they count their change? Is there bargaining, or do they pay a fixed price? Certainly, one of the most enduring concerns has been the integrity of merchants. Consumer distrust seems to have been well founded in many times and places, the scams being remarkably universal. Besides elemental trickery such as giving short change, short weight has been a prime ploy of the unscrupulous. This may be accomplished with the thumb-on-the-scale technique, or by adjusting scales so they misrepresent weight in favor of the seller, or by excessively wetting produce to add ounces of water, or even by weighing a wrapping along with the food itself, a practice not uncommon with items such as sliced smoked salmon, delicatessen meats, fish, and ground beef.

The reliability of the scale, primitively hand-held or electronically calibrated, is equally critical for both canny seller and wary buyer. Nefarious practices are in large part responsible for the appeal supermarkets have to consumers. It must seem a relief to find weights and prices clearly marked on packaged perishables, although that practice still leaves room for cheating.

As with quantity, so with quality, and here adulteration is one of the main tricks. It is most possible with bulk products such as nuts, tea leaves, coffee beans, spices, and the like. It is all too easy to mix high grade with low, the fresh with the stale. Or an inferior product may be misrepresented as superior—cassia passed off as cinnamon, Pennsylvania peaches as those from Georgia, Mexican oregano as Greek, choice beef as prime, flounder fillets as sole. In colonial America, one was literally and figuratively cautioned against sellers of wooden nutmegs, which, much like the admonition not to take any wooden nickels, was a warning against naiveté.

Because it spoils so rapidly and so dangerously, fish has inspired much chicanery. In our modern world, we bemoan the age of the fish we must buy, as boats generally stay out long with their catches, which then travel far from port to market. But in the *Deipnosophists* (Banquet of the Sophists), a lengthy account of manners and customs in Greece during the second century A.D., Athenaeus, the chronicler, expands on the misconduct of fishmongers. He and fellow banquet diners cite "selling fish which is dead and stinking," and sprinkling older specimens with water, "to make the world believe them newly caught and fresh." We have long since adopted Athenaeus's suggestion that the city appoint inspectors of market provisions—a caution practiced in ancient Roman markets. Even so, the Latin message set exquisitely in mosaics at many shop fronts in Rome and Pompeii read *caveat emptor.*

The state of a local economy is obvious in its food markets, too. How well or shabbily are the people dressed, and do they buy food in small quantities or large? Until fairly recently, in Europe food was purchased twice a day in very small quantities—two eggs, an eighth of a pound of butter, half a pint of milk—because electrical current was expensive and refrigerators uncommon. And do merchants display a diversity of good-quality food in abundance, as in the prosperous markets of the United States, Europe, Israel, and Mexico, or are very few pieces set out simply on the ground, as in much of Africa or in the painfully impoverished market of Salvador, Brazil?

Among my more poignant market memories is one of Moscow's Central Market in 1960 when every kind of merchandise was scarce. I watched a large old woman in a heavy black sweater wearing a white babushka that framed her round, cheerless face. She spread newspaper over her section of the counter-table and carefully took out from a paper bag eleven wild black mushrooms, laying them down as meticulously as if they were jewels being placed in Tiffany's window. Nearby a rough-skinned farmer, his gray blanket coat tied with rope, opened a cardboard suitcase packed with excelsior, on top of which he nested twenty-two eggs—his stock for the day.

In a raggle-taggle flea and food market in Bialystok, Poland, amid flurries of wet snow, merchants displayed used kitchen utensils—dented aluminum pots, bent metal mixing spoons, knives with nicked blades—and, nearby, a table held only two long, wide salamis, one flattened in the center as though it had been run over by a car wheel. But customers starved for merchandise were not discouraged, for within ten minutes, all sold out. Unforgettable also in Poland was Warsaw's small Polna Street market, where I observed a hefty woman selling root vegetables. Behind her mounds of parsnips, petrouchka, turnips, and carrots, she sat grating that most incendiary of roots, horseradish. She worked with a grater held over a bowl on her lap, and, with fiery fumes rising, tears streamed down her face, wetting her hot red cheeks that looked like boiled corned beef. I wondered how long she could continue before going blind.

Climate can lend a special character to markets, the more extreme the better. Few in my experience were as mystically beautiful as Helsinki's market, set around its Baltic harbor, one February morning when the temperature was ten below zero. Dressed in so many layers I could not bend my arms at the elbows, and with a ballpoint pen that froze, I walked the thinly populated setting. Florists showed their wares inside trucks through glass back doors, with candles burning between the glass and the flowers to prevent frost, creating a shrinelike effect. Whole fish froze so rapidly that they could be held upright by their tails, shining as though they were glazed ceramics. Shoppers and merchants dashed into tents of orange canvas that glowed warmly, and thawed out over steamy coffee and cuddly cardamom-scented yeast cakes. In contrast, tropical heat and humidity intensify the already strong aromas exuding from preserved fish in the markets of Southeast Asia, where palm trees shield the stalls from the sun and market denizens wear scant, colorful clothing of cotton and silk.

Food itself can be spectacularly memorable, none more so than the whole sides of pigskin, fried in one piece and hanging in Mexican markets like enormous sheets of gold leaf until they are broken into *chicharrónes,* or the intricately arranged candy and fruit offerings to the gods one sees in Bali's markets. Quantity can be stunning, too. In Guangzhou's Qingping, boxes holding heaps of ginger stretch the equivalent of at least two New York City blocks. And hundreds of frozen torpedo-shaped tuna in Tokyo's Tsukiji market are laid out for buyers' inspection, suggesting an airfield full of fighter planes. I thought that must be enough ginger (or tuna) to feed the entire country for a year, but realized each was merely the stock for one day, in one of many markets.

If it is true that markets are designed to accommodate the foods they sell, it is equally true that certain foods can be altered from their natural states to accommodate exigencies of the market. Large chain stores with enormous volume and central warehousing of stock that is reshipped to stores in many different locations require the sturdiest perishables possible. To meet this need, plant engineers such as botanists and horticulturists develop strains that will not ripen too quickly or bruise too easily, yet with enough eye appeal to sell themselves. Not content with crossing strains within the same species, they are now crossbreeding between different species to satisfy mass merchandisers, a futuristic technique resulting in what detractors dub *Frankenfood.* Tomatoes have been prime targets for alteration, leading to the flavorless monstrosity known as the hard-ripe, and the not-yet-realized square tomato meant to fit neatly in cartons and not roll off shelves.

For maximum profits, supermarket varieties of fruits are engineered to absorb enough water while growing to make them "weigh heavy," but not so much that they will spoil rapidly. In contrast, small, less commercial farmers' markets, like many in this book, stock local strawberries, tomatoes, cantaloupes, and the like that are delivered carefully by the growers themselves. Such produce would be too perishable for large commercial markets. In fairness, it should be noted that devotees of organic foods not only tolerate imperfections, but seem romantically to value them—the worm in the apple being a sign that all's natural with the world. If American supermarkets seem like the villains here, be assured that they are only the first. Similar adjustments are gradually coming to supermarkets everywhere.

The concept of a centralized market, though seemingly modern, dates back to ancient times, to the Greek agora and to imperial Rome, where the emperor Trajan established on the Quirinal Hill, next to the Forum, a vast mutileveled market building housing each type of food in its own section. Often food markets were set among other markets for textiles or leather or jewelry, or amid government offices and banks or money changers. "Virtually all medieval cities grew up around a market or a fair, or both," writes Mark Girouard in his social and architectural history *Cities & People*, as he describes some of the famous bygone markets of Florence, Genoa, Venice, Antwerp, and Salisbury. Describing English markets of the fourteenth century, he notes, "The line between wholesaling and retailing was seldom sharply drawn; almost all wholesalers were prepared to sell retail as well." Or vice versa, as every good New Yorker knows.

Finally, the term "market" here refers to a complex of independent merchants gathered within defined premises, indoors or out, under the auspices of a local government or an entrepreneur who owns or rents the space, provides common services, and oversees market practices. Some offer a great variety of foods, while others specialize in a single category such as fish, spices, or truffles. Therefore, we excluded many famous and dazzling markets that have various departments under one ownership: Fauchon in Paris, Harrods in London, Dallmyers in Munich, Dean and DeLuca and Balducci's in New York. Exceptions to such definitions are market streets, such as the Rue Mouffetard in Paris, where a concentration of individually owned shops comprise, in a sense, a market.

Because markets deal with food and food is life, there are many human dimensions that come into play in the marketplace, and you'll find intimations of them all in this book. Consider: the purely elemental bread-alone need to survive; the generosity of spirit as one prepares food for a loved one; the need for the merchant to realize a profit, contrasted with the customer's desire to be frugal; and the lives of market workers who must rise well before dawn, fitting their own family obligations into bizarre schedules. Not least in importance, there are the spiritual concerns of the many market workers who pray before each day's opening, hang pictures of saints and seers in their shops, and place amulets on themselves—or even on their fish—to see them through the day profitably and safely.

ASIA

Asia

Exotic is the word that comes most often to Westerners' minds as they view the teeming, noisy, and odorous markets of the ever-alluring Far East. Visitors today are staggered by the sheer numbers of people and the enormous variety of foods, just as Marco Polo was in the thirteenth century. In the city of Kin-Sai, the present-day Hangzhou, the explorer marveled at no fewer than ten market squares, dazzled by the array of game, fruits, herbs, vegetables, and wine. Of the fish markets he wrote, "At the sight of such vast quantities of sea and lake fish, it would seem impossible to sell all, but within a few hours, all is gone, so great is the number of inhabitants. . . ." That could also be the description of modern Asian fish markets and, most of all, Tsukiji, Tokyo's sprawling wholesale market that might well be called "Seafood City."

Even today, when so many Asian foods (most especially vegetables) have found their way to the world's markets and tables, there are ingredients that set the mind and palate reeling. Throughout China and Southeast Asian countries such as Vietnam, Thailand, Malaysia, and Indonesia, strange foods and spices are purveyed in markets as medicinal cures, none more lurid in appearance than the dried skins of snakes and flattened turtle bodies, and all manner of brown twisted roots and barks. Perhaps even the fabled eye of newt, that literary ingredient of wizardry, might also be in stock. Whether for everyday meals or special celebrations such as the New Year, market stalls display parchment-crisp and translucent desiccated fish stomachs, abalone, and sharks' fins, as well as flattened, leathery animal kidneys, lungs, and bladders.

In contrast to such accessible temptations as hanging slabs of roasted ducks, chickens, and pork with a red-gold lacquer glaze are the more esoteric treats, such as the thousand-year-old eggs with their ashen patina. In fact, they are rarely more than ten weeks old and have been "aged" in a bed of lime clay that imparts a charcoal blue-green glow to the raw eggs as they mellow to a jellied texture. Peeled, these eggs—preferably those of ducks—taste somewhat like a slightly sulfurous blend of anchovies and black olives and are served in small portions as appetizers or garnishes.

A stall at the market in My Tho features a wide assortment of eggs: chicken, quail, duck, and goose.

Equally exotic and, to the conventional Westerner, far more shocking are the live animals sold for food in Asian markets. Anyone living in a large city where ethnic populations support live poultry markets may have seen ducks, geese, and chickens peering out of crates, but those are usually slaughtered in the market for the purchaser. In China and Southeast Asia it is commonplace to see a customer leaving a market clutching a live chicken with its feet tied together to prevent escape. Even more bizarre to the foreigner are live suckling pigs strung up in cylindrical baskets, as well as cats and dogs in wooden crates. As has often been pointed out, these cats and dogs are not pets, but rather livestock raised to be eaten. Food markets, after all, deal starkly with the realities of life, and thus force one to confront such cultural differences in light of one's own customs and mores.

A small pig on its way to the Dali livestock auction.

The clatter of noise as hawkers and shoppers bargain may be expected, and is an especially jangling cacophony when one has absolutely no understanding of the language spoken. But the clatter of odors in these markets can come as a stifling surprise. Preserved foods have a long tradition in these lands, and fermentation is a time-honored technique, never more fragrant than when applied to fish. Not only do the body parts already mentioned give off an acrid and quintessentially fishy aroma, but the headiest scents come from ripened innards in the sauces called *nam pla* and *nuoc mam*. And then there are the salt-pickled vegetables exuding airs, most especially turnips, cabbage, onions, and garlic, much in the manner of Korean kimchi.

India's markets, although as crowded as those in the rest of Asia, emit the softer sounds of a different language and voice pitch, and more mellow and familiar scents. Color is the real stunner in these markets, with a spice-toned palette of pale sunny mustard, orange turmeric, fiery red paprika, and brassy saffron, as well as the earthy browns of cinnamon, cumin, and allspice. In fact, fabrics worn and sold seem to have been dyed with the spices themselves. Gold-orange is a favorite color: in addition to spices, some market stalls offer highly polished brass bowls, trays, and water jugs that used to be sold by weight; still others sell the much-revered marigolds and, in season, garlands of pale yellow jasmine that sweetly scent the air.

Compared to the other Asian markets included here, those of India hint of the Middle East, not only with the abundance of spices, but also with displays of nuts and the cherished seeds of cardamom, sesame, poppy, pepper, caraway, and the gray-green anise often coated with sugar as a breath sweetener. In some corners of Indian markets one finds vendors of *paan*, the popular digestive of betel nut and flavorings such as coconut, cardamom, aniseed, cloves, and silver leaf wrapped in shiny green betel leaves, intricately cut and folded to order. One chews the *paan* and then spits it out. It is said to be a refreshing sort of snack that temporarily reddens teeth and, some say, has a mildly stimulating effect.

Betel leaves filled with betel nuts, spices, and herbs provide a digestive snack called paan.

Fortunately, and most enticingly, fast-food eating is a big feature in Asian markets, partly because there are so many prepared foods to be purchased for meals at home—a custom already well established during the Chinese Song period (960–1280)—but also because there is a tradition of workers and shoppers on limited budgets satisfying their appetites with small snacks throughout the day. China has to be the best place in the world for this sort of noshing, with choices that include an assortment of steamed and fried dumplings filled with meat, vegetables, shrimp, or crab, not to mention wonders such as the crescent-shaped pot-stickers that are filled with pork and half-steamed, half-fried. Endless lengths of noodles made of wheat, rice, or cellophane mung beans are sold dried or prepared in hot- or mild-flavored sauces. Some wheat-flour noodles are formed right on the street, with dough being pulled and twisted into big hanks, then slapped on a table to splay into hundreds of strands—a theatrical feature in the night markets of Xi'an. Then there are soups, bits of grilled meats, puffy yeast buns enfolding sweet pork or red-bean paste, egg-roll pancakes, stir-fried combinations, fried turnip cakes, and, throughout China and Southeast Asia, the soothing, restorative *congee* or *jook*. This beloved dish consists of rice steamed with broth and flecked with vegetables and chicken, crab, or whatever a budget allows.

Phó, a lusty noodle soup that may be garnished with beef, chicken, shrimp, or vegetables and flavored with lemongrass, cilantro, and chilies, is a staple in the markets of Vietnam. Other temptations include ground shrimp on sugarcane skewers, grilled over charcoal, and banana-leaf packets of steamed sticky rice.

Similarly, noodles in a variety of ways, curried ducks' eggs, and tropical fruits and their juices are standard fare in Indonesia. In Bali, pork *satés* are delicious dipped into a sweet-hot-sour sauce of peanuts, chilies, brown sugar, onions, garlic, and tamarind or lemon juice.

Nuts, seeds, roasted and salted chickpeas, and slabs of freshly baked flatbreads filled with potatoes, vegetables, onions, or meats assuage hunger in Indian markets, along with fried vegetable turnovers, the *pakora* and the *samosa*. A favorite snack around Bombay and throughout the Gujarat state is *bhelpoori*, prepared at open carts. It is a satisfying vegetarian mix of crisply puffed rice, lentils, herbs, onions, chopped vegetables, and crunchy wheat-flour wafers.

Unctuously sticky sweets are also popular, from pastel coconut confections, to the fried dough squiggles, *jalebies*, that glisten with sugar syrup, to the fudge-soft *halwah*, often made of spiced carrots or wheat.

If those are not sweet enough for you, nothing ever will be.

Slim dried noodles are the base ingredient for Indian sweet cakes combined with almonds, pistachios, and honey. A special scale is used to weigh the noodles.

Sweet rice rolled and steamed inside banana leaves is a popular snack in the Can Tho market.

The imposing main market building in Cho Lon, the Chinese section of Ho Chi Minh City (Saigon). In the early morning, before the market officially opens, the surrounding streets are filled with vendors and throngs of people.

Featured Markets

China

* Qufu, Shandong Province —A free market in the birthplace of Confucius
* Chengdu, Sichuan Province—The main market for food and spices in the city center
* Dali, Yunnan Province—A livestock and food market in this city on Erhai Lake
* Fuyang, Zhejiang Province—A small country market in the village of Fuyang, outside Hangzhou
* Beijing—The Tiantan market
* Shanghai—Yuyuan Bazaar, the main city market, selling everything from food to hardware to trinkets

Vietnam

* Mekong Delta—Several markets along the canals of the Mekong Delta, especially in the cities of My Tho, Vinh Long, and Can Tho, the largest being the floating market of Phung-Hiep about twenty-five miles from Can Tho
* Cho Lon, Ho Chi Minh City (formerly Saigon)—Cho Lon (meaning "big market" in Chinese) is the Chinese quarter of the city, where an enormous enclosed market sells everything from shoelaces to herbs to meat; vendors set up around the outside of the building before it opens at 7:30 A.M.

Indonesia

Bali

* Denpasar—The central market, Pasar Badung, a multi-storied building selling food and other goods; also the *pasar malam* (open-air market) nearby
* Ubud—A food and handicraft market in this artists' village north of Denpasar

Java

* Muntilan—A general food market in this town located between Yogyakarta and the Buddhist stupa at Borobudur in central Java
* Tosari—A small market in this village on the slopes of Mt. Bromo in eastern Java

India

* Cochin—The general market in this major fishing port and center for the spice trade located on India's southwest coast
* Gadodia Market, Old Delhi—A wholesale spice market located in a building in an enclosed yard just off the Khari Baoli, the city's center for spices
* Chandni Chowk, Old Delhi—The busiest market in Old Delhi, where endless alleys of stalls run off the main business street

The Chinese Kitchen

Lacking abundant fuel for cooking and often short on protein-rich foods, the Chinese developed the quick-cooking method known as stir-fry. Foods cut into small pieces cook quickly, and small amounts of protein (meat, poultry, fish, eggs) can be stretched with vegetables and rice or noodles to feed many.

Chinese cooking utensils are designed to accomplish this sort of cooking efficiently. The wide bowl-like metal pot, the wok, provides a maximum, curved surface for cooking foods evenly and rapidly, and it also cradles whole fish, facilitates the stir-fry motion, and doubles as a nest for steamers. Ideally, the wok is made of thin cast iron (or these days, perhaps of steel or less satisfactory thinner metals, some with nonstick coatings). The metal ring on which it often sits is an accommodation to burners on Western-style ranges. The Chinese stove has deep well burners that hold round-bottom woks steady. Some woks have single handles, others have ring handles on each side. The wok cover is usually of a lighter, less expensive metal, such as aluminum.

To tend food in the wok, Chinese cooks use long cooking chopsticks and straight-edged, long-handled spatulas and ladles. To quickly remove food from the wok the instant that it is cooked, and to separate solids from liquids, the best utensil is the wire strainer-ladle with a long bamboo handle that comes in several sizes. It is equally handy for Western-style cooking, such as taking vegetables out of boiling water.

Two types of cleavers, a heavy chopper for going through bones and a thin slicer with a double-toned blade, are essential, as is a big wooden chopping block or board.

Round, stackable bamboo steamers (today often made of less gracious aluminum) fit into woks to steam large or small quantities of fish, meats, and vegetables, as well as the varieties of dumplings often served directly from such steamers at dim sum restaurants.

A typical kitchen-supply and hardware store at the market in Chengdu.

Wire-bound clay pots, used for braising meats or brewing rich soups, and the combination brazier-and-soup-pot-with-a-chimney known as a Mongolian hotpot are also standards in Chinese cookware shops.

Rapid cooking demands oils and fats that resist burning at all but the highest temperatures. Lard is often used, especially in the Yunnan Province. Among oils, the most favored are peanut, light and dark sesame, and mild-flavored vegetable oils such as corn. Rapeseed oil is somewhat less expensive but has a rough-edged flavor, making it hard to take for the uninitiated.

In this Beijing market, various oils are sold in plastic bottles that are filled from tin storage barrels.

An array of dried spices in the Beijing market.

Bicycles are a primary means of transport in rural China. It is not uncommon to see ducks, chickens, and even pigs carried away from the market by bicycle.

Shanghai Duck with Star Anise

Crisp duck, whether of the Peking type or simply oven-roasted in the Cantonese style, is so complicated and time-consuming to prepare that it is almost always purchased already prepared in roast-meat shops that also sell slabs of pork, spareribs, and chicken, all hanging like brilliant, glazed sculptures. They are chopped into pieces and further heated as additions to stir-fried dishes or served as cold appetizers. This simple duck dish, aromatic with overtones of star anise, can be done at home.

Look for a 4- to 5-pound fresh (not frozen) duck that is not too fatty. Rinse and dry inside and out. Rub inside with 1 teaspoon Chinese five-spice powder. Place 1 bunch cleaned and trimmed scallions, 1 strip dried tangerine or orange peel, and 3 thin slices peeled ginger in a Dutch oven, preferably oval or one in which the duck fits closely. Add all duck giblets except the liver, 4 star anise cloves, and a mixture of 3 tablespoons sugar, ¾ cup dark soy sauce, 1⅓ cups water, and ½ cup dry sherry. Turn the duck over in the sauce until coated and place it in the pot. Bring sauce to a boil, then simmer covered for about 1½ hours, turning duck several times so it cooks evenly and adding water if sauce evaporates. When the duck is tender, turn off heat and let it cool in the covered pot for about 30 minutes. Remove the duck to a platter and skim the fat from the sauce. Return the duck to the pot and cook in the sauce over medium heat, uncovered, turning frequently so it glazes brown on all sides. Sauce should reduce to about ¾ cup. Carve Western style, spooning sauce over the portions, or follow the Chinese custom of chopping the duck into chunks right through the skin and bones, and using the sauce as a dip. Serve with cut-up giblets, hot or cool. This will serve 6 to 10, depending on the other dishes at the meal and whether it is an appetizer or a main course.

Tomatoes, Asian eggplants, garlic chives, onions, and chili peppers are among the wide variety of produce in this typical Chinese market in Fuyang.

Farmers sell bok choy and other local produce at Fuyang's daily market.

Asian Vegetables

Listed here by their Chinese names, most of these vegetables are seen in markets throughout Asia, as are carrots, onions, scallions, snow peas, watercress, kohlrabi, spinach, and cilantro. When buying cabbages, look for firm, solid white bases at the core. Avoid any with brown spots indicating age and possible moldiness.

✖ Bok Choy (Chinese Cabbage)—Small to large, in tall bunches with dark green ruffled leaves; delicate, baby-size cabbages look like chubby tadpoles; delicious steamed with black mushrooms, a Shanghai classic

✖ Siu Choy (Celery or Napa Cabbage)—Very tall, with bottom stalks of white and very pale yellow-green crinkled leaves; a mild cabbage good in soups and stir-fry dishes; overcooks quickly

✖ Choy Sum (Flowering Cabbage)—White stems, dark green spinachlike leaves, and yellow flowers; a sweet-flavored vegetable, lovely when stir-fried with sesame oil

✖ Yau Choy (Rapeseed Cabbage)—Slender green stems, oval leaves, and small yellow flowers; close to Italian broccoli rabe in flavor; blanch to reduce bitterness

✖ Gai Lan (Chinese Broccoli)—Looks like spinach but tastes like the broccoli its green florets resemble; especially good with chicken and finished with a dark oyster sauce

✖ Juk Gai Choy (Mustard Cabbage)—Looks like a chubby, crinkled head of romaine lettuce; warmly soothing bitterness lends itself to strong sauces, some made with preserved paste and always with oil or lard and plenty of garlic.

✖ Een Choy (Amaranth)—Small, green, spinachlike leaves touched with bright purple at the base, sturdy and rough textured; requires a little more steaming than other Asian greens

✖ Ong Choy (Water Vegetable or Water Spinach)—Delicate, cresslike vegetable with a short season, usually late spring to early summer; simmer with preserved bean curd and garlic

✖ Tung Qwa (Winter Melon)—Large, frosty green melon with pale white flesh and yellow seeds; the classic ingredient in an elegant banquet soup that is steamed and served right in its own decoratively carved shell

✖ Mo Qwa (Fuzzy Melon)—Looks like a mottled, hairy cross between a zucchini and a cucumber, with the mildly bitter overtones of the winter melon

✖ Fu Qwa (Bitter Melon)—Looks like a wrinkled, crinkled cucumber; the woody core and red seeds are not eaten, but the flesh is delicious braised or stir-fried with heavy seasonings

✖ Ai Qwa (Asian Eggplant)—Long, thin, and ranging from pale amethyst to deep black-purple, with fewer seeds and drier flesh than European varieties of eggplant

✖ Bak Dau Gok (Long Beans)—Slim beans growing as long as three feet; a bit tougher than string beans and needing longer cooking time; blanch before stir-frying and toss with ground pork, garlic, and hot chilies

✖ Gau Choy Sum (Flowering Garlic Chives)—Fragrant, slim chives topped by yellow or white buds; used as a garnish or as a vegetable, especially good with eggs and bean-curd dishes; stir-fry yellow chives (a first cousin) with eel for a classic Shanghai dish

This Fuyang vendor appears to be knitting with the noodles she sells.

Congee

Yuan Mei, the celebrated eighteenth-century Chinese gourmet-scholar, regarded rice as the perfect food, to be eaten as plainly as possible, the better to appreciate its own sweet juices. The dish dearest to the hearts of Chinese gastronomes is *congee* or *jook,* a soft, soul-soothing porridge of rice simmered for over an hour in rich chicken broth and served with garnishes such as chicken, fried onions, pickled vegetables (garlic, kohlrabi, or turnips), chopped scallions, or preserved eggs. Also known as chicken rice in the fast-food stalls of markets throughout China and Southeast Asia, *congee* is a morning dish and the last sustaining course in a dim sum breakfast. It is best made with a combination of short-grained rice and glutinous, or sticky, rice, both among the many varieties displayed in sacks and bins in Chinese markets.

A Qufu vendor sells garlic and dried rice dough.

In the sweltering hot market of Qufu, a small city in the Shandong Province, merchants offer components of the typical daily fare: bean sprouts, fried tofu, and dough for noodles.

Hand-held Chinese scales come in a variety of sizes, from small ones that weigh spices and gems to heavier models for bulky items.

Steamed Fish with Ginger and Scallions

This classic Cantonese preparation makes the most of delicate, fresh fish, purchased live. (Frying is reserved for dead fish, albeit fresh.) A whole fish is steamed directly on the serving platter, which is placed inside a wok or a round bamboo steamer set over a wok. Any steamer for vegetables or clams can be used, as can a deep skillet or Dutch oven that has a tight-fitting cover and is large enough to hold the dish.

Look for the freshest, preferably live, 1½- to 2-pound flounder, sea bass, porgy, or similar non-oily, white-fleshed fish, and have it scaled and eviscerated. Head and tail should remain intact. With a sharp, thin-bladed knife, cut three slashes through the skin on each side of the fish. Lay in a heatproof glass or ceramic dish or a deep platter and marinate for 30 minutes at room temperature in a mixture of 2 tablespoons soy sauce, 3 tablespoons dry sherry or rice wine, 1 tablespoon peanut or sesame oil, ⅓ cup brown bean sauce (*mein see*) mashed into the other liquids, 2 tablespoons finely minced fresh ginger, chopped green and white parts of 3 or 4 scallions, 2 minced garlic cloves, and a pinch of sugar. Turn the fish once during marinating. Lay two chopsticks on the bottom of the pot to form a rack, and place the dish on the chopsticks. Fill the pot with enough boiling water to reach the bottom of the dish. Cover the pot and steam the fish over high heat for 10 to 15 minutes, or until the meat flakes off the bone. Serve in the steaming dish placed on a larger cold platter, or slide the fish onto a warm, clean platter, spooning sauce over it. Garnish with slivered raw scallions and drizzle overall 1 tablespoon hot peanut or sesame oil. To serve the fish, remove meat from the top side first, then lift the bone to spoon out the bottom layer. The Chinese consider it unlucky to turn a fish over. Serve with steamed rice. This will serve 2 to 4.

Preserved Fish Products

Protein being an essential element in a healthy diet, it has historically been preserved, in one form or another, in order to keep a steady supply on hand. Some of those forms, such as fermentation, add a distinct flavor to food that becomes habitually preferred, and so the preserved products are used as seasonings as well. In China and Southeast Asia dried fish and fish parts (stomachs, fins, and so on), dried shrimp, and cured sauces, such as the dark *nam pla* and *nuoc mam*—much like the Roman *garum* that was made of fermented fish innards—of Thailand and Vietnam, fill markets with heady stenches that are often stifling to newcomers. The strong flavors and volatile aromas of the two sauces evaporate in cooking, leaving only a gentle overtone of salty fishiness, much like a combination of anchovy paste and Worcestershire sauce.

Left: The chaotic floating market of Phung-Hiep is located at the meeting point of several canals in the Mekong Delta.

An entire section of the market in My Tho is devoted to preserved fish.

Right: In the early-
morning rush, a vendor
pushes her scooter
through the streets of
Ho Chi Minh City
(Saigon).

Suspecting that the best
produce is buried at the
bottom, a Vinh Long
woman digs deep into
a basket of radishes.

Phó-by
Noodle Soup with Beef

The favorite Vietnamese fast-food meal, the nourishing, aromatic, meaty soups called *phó,* after the dried rice noodles they contain, also include beef, pork, poultry, or shrimp, and vegetables. Hot sauce—very hot sauce—is added to taste.

For 4 main-course portions, pour hot water over ½ pound dried rice-stick noodles and soak for 20 minutes, then drain. In a large pot combine 10 cups beef broth and 3 cups water, and simmer with 3 thin slices peeled ginger and 2 peeled garlic cloves for about 10 minutes. Add, to taste, 6 soaked, dried black Chinese mushrooms, ½ head cut-up napa cabbage, 1 head cut-up bok choy, 1 large, thinly sliced onion, 2 small fresh seeded chili peppers, ½ pound snow peas with strings removed, and 3 or 4 sprigs of fresh cilantro. Almost any vegetable is optional; you can also add spinach and cubed fresh white bean curd (about ¼ pound). Season with 1 to 2 teaspoons of Thai or Vietnamese fermented fish sauce (*nam pla* or *nuoc mam*) or a dab of anchovy paste dissolved in 2 teaspoons Worcestershire sauce. Simmer for 10 minutes and adjust seasonings, adding salt if needed. Add drained noodles and cook for about 5 minutes or until done. One-half pound lean raw beef cut into ribbon strips can be simmered for a few seconds in the soup, or can be placed raw over boiling hot soup when it is in individual bowls so that the meat cooks as it is being eaten, rare being the traditional state of doneness. Ladle soup with vegetables and noodles into 4 warm, deep soup bowls. Optional but traditional garnishes include cilantro, mint or basil leaves, chopped scallions, bean sprouts, and slivered green chili peppers. Wedges of lime and hot chili paste are added individually.

A cucumber vendor in My Tho relaxes in his hammock.

Above: The bicycle ranks second only to the boat as the most important mode of transportation in the Mekong Delta. These coconuts have just been unloaded from a canal boat in Vinh Long.

Below: A stall full of bananas and jackfruit.

Southeast Asian Fruits

One easily recognizes fruits such as bananas, pineapples, mangoes, litchis, papayas, coconuts, and kiwis in Southeast Asian markets, but there are a number of more unusual varieties, some also common to South America with its similar climate.

* Asian Pear—Also known as Chinese pear or, in Japanese, *nashi;* looks like an apple with the bronze skin of a Bosc pear and tastes like a watery, hard pear; an icy-crisp and refreshing fruit
* Breadfruit—Large, round, and with green skin mottled in a "brain" pattern; used as a vegetable, with an elusive flavor: uncooked, suggesting raw potato; cooked, taking on the soft sweetness of eggplant perhaps mixed with potato
* Durian—Big green melons covered with porcupinelike spikes that give fair warning of the frankly putrid aroma within, with soft yellow flesh smelling overpoweringly of overripe Camembert combined with cauliflower, exactly the qualities devotees cherish
* Djeruk-manis—Small, green citrus fruits from Sumatra; sweet-tart and juicily thirst-quenching
* Jackfruit—A melonlike fruit with a mild cheese flavor; an Indonesian favorite usually cooked in slices with coconut milk and spices as a side dish called *gudeg*
* Loquat—Also known as Japanese plum; a small, oval golden fruit with a large, shiny brown seed; juicy and delicately sweet-tart; usually has unavoidable brown spots that should not affect quality if skin is intact; sold canned for use in fruit salads
* Pomelo—Large, thick-skinned, pink-yellow citrus fruit, much like grapefruit, ranging from sweet to bitter, pungent to bland
* Rakam—Small, delicate Thai strawberries
* Rambutan—A cheery, spiky red fruit with a soft acidic pulp, usually eaten out of hand but also added to fruit salads
* Star Fruit or Carambola—A long and deeply ridged form with a waxy yellow skin; cuts into star-shaped slices that are gently acidic; more decorative than delicious
* Tamarillo—Also called a tree tomato; small, shiny oval fruit with skin ranging from crimson to golden yellow, and with soft flesh and a circle of purplish seeds within; very tart and best simmered with sugar into a relish or chutney

At the Cho Lon market, a young woman sells rosy rambutan from her bicycle.

Left: A market along a canal near Can Tho.

Right: A Can Tho fish merchant rushes to his stall with a block of ice.

If it happens to be a market day in the village, at dawn
the roads are crowded with husky people from the
near-by villages who come to sell their products—piles
of coconuts, bananas, or vegetables, pottery, mats, baskets,
and so forth. . . . If there is a feast in the village temple,
the people parade in yellow, green and magenta silks
with fantastic pyramids of fruit and flowers, offerings
to the gods, in a pageant that would have made Diaghilev
turn green with envy. . . . Most markets have a little shrine
for the goddess of fertility and of gardens, Dewi Melanting,
also the deity of the market, to whom the vendors make
small offerings for good luck.

—From *Island of Bali* by Miguel Covarrubias

*Before sunrise,
a Balinese woman
carefully chooses
leaves to use in her
morning offering.*

*Seen from above,
between rattan sun
shades, an offering to
the gods sits atop a pile
of chili peppers in the
market at Ubud, a village
outside Denpasar.*

57

Saté Babi

Balinese Pork Saté with Peanut-Chili Sauce

Saté, *skewered meat with various spices grilled over an open fire, is a popular dish in Balinese markets. It is served with a pungent sauce.*

Saté is standard fare in Indonesian markets. Balinese people, being Hindus, make theirs of pork or poultry, but never of beef. Muslims in the rest of Indonesia shun pork and favor beef. Either type of meat (or lamb, veal, chicken, or duck) makes delicious *saté*, best grilled over charcoal. *Saté* works well as an appetizer or as part of a *nasi padang*, the Indonesian name for the meal Dutch colonists dubbed *rijsttafel*—many cooked dishes served around rice. The sweet and pungent *saté* dip is equally good with grilled foods such as spareribs, shrimp, and chicken. All of the authentic ingredients can be found in Asian markets or gourmet shops, but substitutes are suggested.

Cut 1½ pounds lean, tender pork into ½-inch cubes. Blend 2 teaspoons Thai or Indonesian shrimp paste or 1 teaspoon anchovy paste into 3 tablespoons water. Mix with 2 grated candlenuts (do not taste these raw) or 2 grated unsalted macadamia nuts, 2 minced garlic cloves, 3 tablespoons sweet soy sauce, and 3 tablespoons peanut oil. Pour over pork and marinate for 2 hours. Thread cubes onto wet bamboo skewers, sliding them close together but not cramming them tightly. Broil over red-hot charcoal or in a preheated broiler, turning once or twice until meat is done, about 7 minutes.

Fresh peanut sauce (*kacang baru*) can be made in advance and kept in the refrigerator for several days. Sauté 1 medium chopped onion and 3 minced garlic cloves in 2 or 3 tablespoons peanut oil, as needed. When brown, add to the bowl of a food processor with 2 cups shelled and roasted unsalted peanuts, a 2-inch strip of lemongrass, 2 thin slices of peeled ginger, 1½ tablespoons Thai or Indonesian shrimp paste or 1 tablespoon anchovy paste, 1 small fresh seeded red or green chili pepper, 2 teaspoons palm sugar or brown sugar, 2 tablespoons dark soy sauce, 3 tablespoons tamarind or lemon juice, and salt to taste. Purée until smooth, trickling in just enough boiling water to make a dippable but still clinging paste.

The public market in Denpasar. The name of the Balinese capital means "east of the market."

Women in Bali often carry towering bundles on their heads.

*The large general market
in Muntilan is located between
Yogyakarta and the Buddhist stupa
at Borobudur in central Java.*

Rogan Gosht
Aromatic Lamb Curry

Turcurri, or what we know as curry, is a stew seasoned with a spice blend most often purchased already mixed. But authentic Indian cooks prefer to blend their own curry powders, combining spices that go best with the intended fish, poultry, meat, or vegetable dish.

Heat 2 tablespoons unsalted butter and 2 tablespoons corn oil in a heavy, 3-quart casserole and sauté 1 cup chopped onion to a rich golden brown. Stir in 2 pounds lean, boneless lamb cut from the leg into 1- to 1½-inch cubes. Stir in 1 tablespoon turmeric, 2 tablespoons powdered coriander, ½ teaspoon powdered cumin, ½ teaspoon ground black pepper, a pinch or two of cayenne pepper, 2 teaspoons powdered cardamom, and 1 tablespoon finely minced fresh ginger. Fry and stir for a minute or two until spices lose their raw smell. Stir in 1 cup plain yogurt and simmer over very low heat, stirring frequently, for about 45 minutes or until lamb is almost done. Add water or a little skim milk during cooking if needed to prevent scorching. Add 3 medium-size boiling potatoes, peeled and cut into 1-inch cubes, and continue cooking for 30 to 40 minutes until potatoes and meat are very soft, adding water as needed. Top with slivered, blanched almonds and serve with rice. This makes 6 to 8 servings, depending on the other dishes at the meal.

Garam Masala
The Classic Indian Spice Mix

Piled in cone-shaped peaks atop barrels, heaped in mounds in burlap sacks, spices are the colorful stars of Indian markets, where one finds, perhaps, the world's greatest array. Rather than buy the already mixed combinations now increasingly available, the most careful cook buys whole spices, roasts them before peeling or shelling, and grinds them as the basis of garam masala. Used as a final seasoning, the most basic garam masala combines cinnamon, cloves, black pepper, and cardamom; coriander seeds and cumin are also added sometimes, alone or in combination. Buy spices in small quantities and replace them often so they will retain their bright color, flavor, and aroma. Whole spices stay fresh longer than the ground and should be stored in a cool place, away from light, as they contain oils that turn rancid.

Spice stalls abound in Delhi's markets.

Sorting red beans in a small street stall in Delhi.

Tamatar Chutni

Tomato Chutney

Buy 2 pounds of tomatoes that are some-what ripe but still firm. Cut tomatoes in half crosswise and gently squeeze them over the sink to remove seeds and excess juice. Chop coarsely, eliminating core end. Place in a 3-quart enameled or stainless-steel saucepan along with a pinch of the Indian spice mix *punch-phoron,* which combines tiny pinches each of powdered cumin, black cumin, mustard, fennel, fenugreek, cinnamon, and cloves. Add 2 tablespoons finely minced, peeled ginger, 3 peeled and chopped garlic cloves, 1 or 2 small, fresh red or green chilies without their seeds, 1/3 cup cilantro leaves, 1 1/2 cups chopped onion, 1 cup cider or malt vinegar, 2 tea-spoons salt, and 1 cup dark brown sugar. Bring to a boil and then simmer gently for 10 minutes, stirring frequently. Stir in 2/3 cup hot mustard or vegetable oil and 3 tablespoons black mustard seeds. Simmer very gently for about 10 more minutes, or until chutney is thick. Adjust seasonings. Cool, pack in a glass or ceramic container (this makes about 3 cups in all), cover tightly, and refrigerate. The chutney will keep for 2 to 3 weeks.

Above: Waiting for customers.

*Below: On Chandni Chowk, Old Delhi's busiest
market street, a vendor arranges her vegetables.*

At the entrance to the Gadodia wholesale spice market,
just off the Khari Baoli in Old Delhi, the crush of pushcarts
and porters creates a traffic jam.

*Brightly colored
carrots and lotus
roots for sale
in Delhi.*

In Delhi, fresh chickpeas are sold both raw and gently parboiled to bring out their bright green coloring.

Gingered Chickpeas

You will need 3 cups cooked chickpeas: use either the canned variety or dried chickpeas that have been soaked and cooked in lightly salted water. If you use canned chickpeas, turn them into a strainer and rinse under cold running water to remove canning liquid. In 2 tablespoons unsalted butter and 2 tablespoons corn oil, lightly brown 1 cup chopped onion and 3 minced garlic cloves. Stir in 1 tablespoon minced peeled ginger, $1\frac{1}{2}$ teaspoons turmeric, and a generous pinch each of powdered coriander and cayenne and black peppers. Add 2 medium-size seeded and drained chopped tomatoes or $\frac{2}{3}$ cup drained canned crushed tomatoes, and cook until mixture thickens. Stir in chickpeas with 1 tablespoon lemon juice, a pinch or two of salt as needed, and $\frac{1}{2}$ cup water. Simmer slowly, covered, for about 10 minutes or until thick. Adjust seasonings. Serve warm, garnished with thin onion slices, slivered green chilies, lemon wedges, and mint leaves. This can be stored in the refrigerator for 3 or 4 days and is best reheated in the top of a double boiler.

Porters line up awaiting work at the Gadodia market in Old Delhi.

Cochin, on the southwest coast of India, has been a major center of the spice trade for centuries. A pile of ginger dries in a warehouse in Fort Cochin.

EUROPE

Europe

Europe's characteristic diversity is as discernible in its food markets as it is in its languages, currencies, manners, and customs. All change dramatically as one crosses over, for example, from France into Germany or Italy. Despite the basic similarity of available fruits and vegetables, with only minor variations to accommodate local preferences and native products, the markets of these countries, as well as those of Spain, England, Finland, and the rest of Europe, vary in tone, style, behavior, method of display, and, not the least, noise level.

The coolly beautiful order of Helsinki's harbor market, where anyone attempting to haggle would be branded an outsider, is in sharp contrast to the self-entertainment provided by both vendors and customers jockeying for advantage on the raffish docks of Marseilles or in the seaside market of Pozzuoli, outside of Naples. European produce, cheeses, and poultry may be in danger of losing their identities due to uniform standards imposed by the European Economic Community, but the diversity of the cast should remain remarkably intact.

The French taste and finesse in all aspects of gastronomy are obvious in the exquisitely arranged food stalls of that country, whether in the individual shops lined up along market streets, such as at the dazzling juncture of the Rue de Seine and the Rue de Buci or on the Rue Mouffetard in Paris; or along the Cours Saleya in Nice, with its tree-shaded, Impressionistic shimmer; or in covered markets, such as the intimate Marché St. Germain in Paris or the vast Les Halles de la Part-Dieu in Lyons.

Most colorful in our modern world, and still going strong despite the invasion of *hypermarchés,* are France's roving markets—*marchés volants* —also a custom in some parts of Italy. These itinerants set up on regular schedules in various cities and towns, and, according to Patricia Wells in *The Food Lover's Guide to Paris,* there are almost sixty such markets in that city alone.

Before mass communication, vendors in these markets purveyed news of the surrounding regions, feeding the appetite for gossip as much as for fresh comestibles. It is magical to watch the activity in the pale light

Previous pages: A decaying old building serves as a backdrop for a vegetable stand in Palermo's Ballarò market.

Small, high-quality radishes are in great demand at the market in Lyons.

of morning, as truck doors are flung open at the side or rear, canopies are stretched across frames to ward off the elements, and mouthwatering temptations, including all sorts of perishables, are intricately laid out, scenting the air with nose-twitching enticements. Just as magically, after lunchtime the culinary carnival packs up and moves on.

As might be expected in France, there is a good deal of delectable snacking possible in all of these markets. Wherever oysters are sold, there will be an oyster bar offering the elegantly saline Belons, the satiny and salty green Marennes, the racy if unrefined Portuguese, and, with luck, the celebrated Armoricaines of Brittany. A drop of lemon juice or the shallot-and-wine-vinegar *sauce mignonnette* and a glass of Chablis are all the accompaniments necessary for total satisfaction. Small cafés—*salons de dégustation*—featuring simple dishes of market products abound also in the urban and larger covered markets, and there are always chunks of bread, cuts of cheese, ripe fruit, and slices of apple tart for after-market picnics.

Germany's markets by contrast are quieter and have an orderly, immaculate glow that in no way makes them less tempting, whether the setting is modern, such as the stupendous spread in Berlin's KaDeWe (Kaufhaus des Westens) department store, or traditional, as in the Viktualienmarkt—"Food, or Victuals, Market"— in the heart of Munich. One finds a sparkling array of fruits and vegetables, breads and cheeses, flowers and herbs, honey ladled out of hive-shaped vats, meats, poultry, game, fresh and smoked fish, and, most typically, ropes and garlands of the famed Bavarian wursts: snowy veal *Weisswürste* that is steamed; coarser pork bratwurst that is fried, as its name implies; red and spicy, long thin *Polnischers;* and the pungent, rough-textured *Regensburger,* to name only a few.

A Provençal cheese vendor does his best to attract customers.

Pyramids of giant white radishes, sturdy orange-red carrots, and waxy white and green leeks; globes of red, green, and white cabbage; turnips from small, violet-tinged globes to giant golden rutabagas; and potatoes in all sizes are the standards of Munich's popular market. Some of the wares are sold outdoors under umbrellas and canopies, many sporting the Bavarian state colors: blue and white. In winter, transparent plastic panels protect those stalls from the elements; as the tents become misted with steam on the inside, they take on a dreamy, underwater quality.

Market workers and early shoppers breakfast at the many beer taverns, or *Brauhaus,* rimming the marketplace to quaff powerful *Münchener Weissbier*—Munich white beer—its pale sunniness accented by a dash of lemon juice. They sip as they wait for liver dumplings in broth, eggs scrambled with wurst and potatoes, or *Beinfleisch,* the beloved local boiled beef. Outdoors the air is pungent with the scents of faster sustenance: grilling wurst, the steamy hot pâté called *Leberkäse,* piquant sauerkraut, and Bavaria's sweet and sprightly mustard.

In Italian markets, as one might expect, the decibles mount, the action speeds up, and passions are all on the surface. This is certainly true of the three neighboring markets winding through alleys in the center of the Sicilian capital, Palermo—Mercato della Vucciria, Capo, and Ballarò. The first is the oldest and most operatic. Of all the explanations for its name, "vociferous" seems the most likely. The cacophony of voices and screams is joyously deafening, as vendors hawk their wares, customers bargain, mothers call for children, and children call for something to eat and are silenced with a slice of pizza topped with herbed tomatoes. Many men shop at Palermo's markets for their families, a courtesy to women who are busy at home, according to Giuliano Bugialli in his *Foods of Sicily and Sardinia.* All this occurs against a

In Munich, dried meats, ham, and sausages are bought to be eaten at home or with a piece of bread as a take-away sandwich.

jam-packed assortment of foodstuffs, shaded from the sun by red awnings that cast a rosy light over the proceedings. Produce arrives by donkey cart, truck, or on the heads of porters.

The most stunning areas are devoted to black, green, purple, and walnut-brown olives; dried condiments such as hot peppers and the salt-cured capers from Pantelleria; and, above all, seafood such as gigantic tunas and trophy swordfish. Freshness is the prize, with many small fish curled head to tail, indicating that rigor mortis has not yet subsided. Despite that and the salty, sea-fresh scent in the air, shoppers sniff carefully, peer into the gills looking for bright blood-redness, and press the skin with their fingertips to see if the flesh bounces back.

There is less snacking in Italian markets than in others of Europe, but to keep body and soul together there is—in addition to pizza and focaccia—fruit, cheese, sandwiches made in the various *salumerie* selling sausages and pickled vegetables, and, never far away anywhere in Italy, a tiny cup half-filled with midnight-dark espresso. Never very far away in Sicily is a

In the market of Palermo's old Capo district, a vendor shows off his artfully arranged green cauliflower.

pasticceria for a cannoli or two, or a *gelateria* where thick, creamy, egg-enriched ice cream is served *in briocha*, sandwiched into a puffy brioche.

There is no such thing as a typical market in Europe—indeed, within Italy alone. For if Italy's markets differ widely from those of France and Germany, so does the Vucciria differ from the restrained, seasonal truffle market of Alba in the northern region of Piedmont, or the relatively sedate San Lorenzo covered market in Florence, or the romantically mellow Verona market in the antique Piazza delle Erbe—the aptly named "Vegetable Square."

Featured Markets

France

✳ Rue Mouffetard, Paris—A lively market street where there is much haggling over prices and quality

✳ Dupleix, Paris—One of the numerous roving markets that set up in different neighborhoods on specific days, here on the Boulevard de Grenelle

✳ Trouville-sur-Mer—An afternoon fish market at the wharf in this Normandy resort town

✳ Lyons—A Sunday farmers' market on the Quai des Célestins

✳ Velleron—A typical Provençal farmers' market in a parking lot in this town on the Sorgue River

Germany

✳ Viktualienmarkt, Munich—The immaculate, picturesque daily market held in the city center since 1807

✳ Christkindlmarkt, Munich—Typical of the "Christ-child markets" held throughout Germany and Austria from Advent to Christmas Eve; here on the Marienplatz

Italy

✳ Mercato del Tartufo, Alba—The market for the Piedmont region's renowned, highly fragrant black and white truffles; held daily, October through December

✳ Mercato della Vucciria, Capo Market, and Ballarò Market, Palermo—Operatic markets in the Sicilian capital offering all sorts of food; held every day except Sunday

✳ Pisa—A busy market tucked into the small alleyways of this Tuscan town

✳ Trieste—The market in the Piazza Ponte Rosso, a main square in this Adriatic seaport in the Friuli-Venezia Giulia region

The weekly market in the Piazza Ponte Rosso in Trieste.

One can't impose unity on a country that has 265 different cheeses.

—Attributed in various forms to several sources,
including Winston Churchill and Charles de Gaulle,
and with cheeses numbering more than 350

*Delicious chèvre—France's famous goat cheese—is made in small batches
by a number of farmers who bring their products to the Lyons market.*

Bread

Le pain se lève—"the bread is rising"—was the secret password among citizens conspiring to storm the Bastille. Shortages of bread have caused riots in the streets of many countries at many times, none more famous than the French Revolution. Whether the French value bread more than others is arguable; what is certain is that they have turned bread-baking into a fine art and have created many subtle variations for different meals and foods. The classic image of France, in fact, is of a small boy or girl in a school smock carrying a long, thin, crusty baguette home from the *boulangerie*.

A generation ago, great bread could be taken for granted everywhere in France. Now, alas, progress and the demands of modern production and economics have taken a toll. As the couturier Christian Lacroix said when describing the state of bread and croissants in France, "Today, to get the best, you must have an address."

Chèvres

Goat cheeses

As staggering as the total number of French cheeses may be, an observation made even by the Roman naturalist Pliny the Elder, it is even more sobering, perhaps, to realize that there are almost one hundred made of goat's milk alone. As classified and illustrated in the definitive directory *French Cheeses,* by Kazuko Masui and Tomoko Yamada, French chèvres range from mild and creamy to hard-crusted and stingingly sharp, some with only the mildly acidic tinge of fresh goat's milk, others scented with herbs or moldy oak or chestnut leaves, and still others burnished with soft, salty gray-black ashes.

The aroma of freshly baked bread permeates Paris's Dupleix market along the Boulevard de Grenelle.

You are eating the sea, that's it, only the sensation of a gulp of sea water has been wafted out of it by some sorcery, and you are on the verge of remembering you don't know what, mermaids or the sudden smell of kelp on the ebb tide or a poem you read once, something connected with the flavor of life itself . . .

—On tasting Brittany's
Armoricaines oysters, from
The Oysters of Locmariaquer
by Eleanor Clark

*A fishmonger in Trouville-sur-Mer,
a resort town in Normandy,
proudly displays a skate.*

*Fresh fish and shellfish are
features of the Lyons market
on the Quai des Célestins.*

Moules au Gratin

Baked Herbed Mussels

Celebrated for such deep-sea provender as sole, turbot, mackerel, langoustine, oysters, and shrimp, Normandy is also much appreciated for its shiny, briny mussels that garnish many fish dishes. In this savory dish, they play a solo starring role. Shop for mussels with tightly closed shells indicating they are alive, and avoid those that are broken or feel heavy for their size as they are probably full of sand. In these days of polluted waters, it is best to buy farmed mussels, even though they are blander than the wild.

To serve 6 appetizer portions, buy about 4 pounds (about 5 quarts) of clean, bright mussels. Soak in ice water for 1 hour, then scrub with a stiff brush and scrape off the threadlike beards. Steam covered in a wide and deep skillet in 1 cup water for about 7 or 8 minutes, or until all open, shaking pot once or twice. Discard any mussels that do not open, as well as the top shell of each opened mussel. Strain the liquid through a fine sieve or a paper coffee filter and reserve. Blend 1 pound softened unsalted butter with 2 tablespoons finely minced shallots, $^2/_3$ cup minced parsley, $^1/_2$ teaspoon dried or 1 tablespoon minced fresh thyme, 1 teaspoon salt, a pinch of black pepper, and 1 tablespoon Calvados. Thin the mixture to spreading consistency with some of the reserved cooking liquid. Top the mussels on halfshells with the butter filling. Arrange in a single layer in one or two shallow baking pans in the upper third of a preheated 425-degree oven for 7 or 8 minutes, or until herb butter has melted and the tops are faintly golden. Divide onto warm appetizer plates and serve with slices of French bread, so none of the precious butter will be wasted.

Faisan en Cocotte

Braised Pheasant

A vendor at the Dupleix market in Paris sells wild game, pâtés, and other prepared foods.

Butchers at the roving street market offer all sorts of prepared dishes in addition to the traditional fare, including paellas, savory tarts, charcuterie, and fragrant terrines.

Pheasant, like most game birds found in our markets, tends to be dry and bland, and though it can be roasted to a nut-brown finish, it is more supple and succulent when braised. Choose a 2- to 2½-pound wild or farmed pheasant to serve 2 people. Singe if necessary (to remove feather residue) and sprinkle a little brandy in the cleaned cavity. Drain and rub cavity with salt and pepper and insert a sprig or two of fresh thyme. Rub the outside with salt and pepper and tie the bird with kitchen string so the legs and wings stay in place. In a small, heavy, and deep casserole just large enough to hold the pheasant, heat 2 tablespoons unsalted butter and 1 tablespoon diced lean bacon or rinsed salt pork. Brown pheasant slowly on all sides, then remove. Add to pan ½ chopped onion, 1 finely diced carrot, and 2 minced shallots. Sauté until pale golden, then pour in about 3 tablespoons brandy. Raise heat so the brandy evaporates. Place pheasant on its side over the vegetables, and add ½ cup white wine. Bring to a boil, cover, and reduce heat to simmer gently but steadily for 45 minutes to 1 hour, turning once or twice so pheasant cooks evenly. Add water if vegetables become dry. When pheasant is tender, remove it, cut off strings, and reserve in a warm corner. Strain pan juices into a saucepan, rubbing through the strainer as much of the vegetables as possible. Skim fat from the sauce; adjust seasonings and reheat. Cut the pheasant in quarters and serve a thigh and breast quarter to each person, spooning the reduced sauce over the pieces. Serve with braised cabbage and mashed or roasted potatoes, or wild rice. For an extra elegant touch, slip two or three thin slices of black truffle under the skin along breasts and thighs before you season and tie the bird.

An extravagant display of tomatoes, asparagus, haricots verts, white-tipped radishes, and berries on the Rue Mouffetard, one of the older and most popular market streets in Paris.

The busy market in Velleron, a town in Provence along the Sorgue River, begins in the afternoon.
Farmers arrange leeks and other produce on tables in front of their trucks.

Homemade apple tarts are a favorite treat at the Lyons market.

Tarte aux Pommes

Apple Tart

Fairly sweet apples are traditional for this classic open tart. To ensure success, buy about 2½ pounds relatively dry apples such as Northern Spy, or Red or Yellow Delicious. Peel, core, and slice apples vertically—thinly and evenly—and sauté in 4 tablespoons butter until slices are a pale golden brown. Sprinkle slices with 1 tablespoon sugar and a few drops of Calvados or Armagnac. Set aside, reserving juices. Set an 8- to 9-inch flan ring on a baking sheet. Prepare enough soft, short pie-crust pastry (with butter and a pinch of sugar) to fit the ring; you will not use a top crust. Roll out the dough and line the ring. Arrange overlapping slices of apple in a concentric circle. Do not add juice yet. Brush rim of pie crust with a little heavy sweet cream. Bake in a preheated 425-degree oven for 25 to 30 minutes, rotating pan if tart is not browning evenly. Slide tart out of oven and pour in reserved juices. Bake 2 or 3 minutes more. Serve hot, warm, or cold.

Christkindlmarkt

During the four weeks between Advent and Christmas Eve, almost every German and Austrian town (most notably, Munich, Nuremberg, Vienna, and Salzburg) glows with a Christkindlmarkt—a "Christ-child market." These markets are festive with carol singing, fragrant with the perfume of clove-scented hot wine known as *Glühwein*, and bursting with holiday gifts and decorations, Christmas spice cookies, marzipan candies, and toy figures of St. Nicholas and the devil Krampus formed of wired prunes. Located in the Marienplatz, in the shadow of the nineteenth-century Neues Rathaus (New City Hall) with its playful glockenspiel, Munich's market is especially famous for its *Krippen*, nativity scene figures that are crafted in every size and material. The most stunning figures are in wood, as one might expect in the land of master woodcarver Tilman Riemenschneider (1460?–1531). Magical by night when colored lights shimmer through the snow-frosted air, Munich's Christmas market is Germany's oldest, with more than six hundred years of revelry to its credit.

*Munich's annual
Christkindlmarkt
is held in the
Marienplatz.*

A dream for Hansel and Gretel: a sweet shop filled with cookies, decorations, and other Christmas treats.

Zimtsterne

Cinnamon Stars

These aromatic symbols of Christmas are always among the *Weihnachtsgebäck,* or Christmas baking, that begins in many German households right after Advent. They are especially good accompaniments to the spicy, red-hot wine punch, *Glühwein.* Both are bracing restoratives sold in the frosty German and Austrian Christkindlmarkts.

Beat the whites of 3 extra-large eggs until foamy and thick, then gradually beat in 1¼ cups sugar. Beat until whites form stiff, white, shiny peaks. Set aside ½ cup of the beaten whites. Sprinkle remaining whites with 1 tablespoon cinnamon, 1½ cups grated, unblanched almonds, ½ teaspoon almond extract, and 1 teaspoon brandy. Stir together thoroughly but gently. The mixture should be fairly solid, much like thick oatmeal. Add more almonds until the dough can be rolled. (You may need as much as 1½ pounds in all.) Sprinkle a pastry board lightly with sugar or grated nuts and, with a rolling pin, roll dough to ¼-inch thickness. With a 1½- to 2-inch star-shaped cookie cutter, cut cookies. Arrange on one or several buttered baking sheets, leaving about a ½-inch space between each star. Brush the top of each cookie with a little of the reserved egg whites. Bake in a preheated 300-degree oven for about 20 minutes or until pale golden. Cool completely on racks before storing in airtight tin boxes. This makes about 6 dozen cookies.

The variety of potatoes sold in Germany is probably the widest in Europe. A small shop in the Viktualienmarkt is devoted exclusively to potatoes.

Bayrische Wintergemüsesuppe
Bavarian Winter Vegetable Soup

Root vegetables, tubers, and cabbages keep well in cold weather and are simmered up into many flavorful winter dishes, none more satisfying than this hearty Bavarian soup. Be sure root vegetables and tubers are firm with no withering, soft spots, or mold. To feed four hungry winter appetites, buy a 2-pound head of green or white cabbage (one with a stem bottom that is firm and white), 3 medium-size carrots, 2 or 3 medium-size leeks, 1 medium-size onion, 2 small white turnips or kohlrabi, 2 large boiling potatoes, and any other root vegetables you like, such as ½ a parsnip, 1 parsley root, or ½ a small knob celery. Shred cabbage. Peel all vegetables and cut them into spoon-size pieces or half-rounds. Place in a 4- to 5-quart soup pot and cover with 8 to 10 cups water, or beef or chicken broth, or a combination of these liquids. Add ½ teaspoon dried marjoram, 1 small bay leaf, 1 teaspoon salt, and 8 to 10 black peppercorns. Bring to a boil, reduce to a simmer, and cook, partially covered, until all the vegetables are very tender, about 30 minutes. Replenish water to original level during cooking. Soup develops flavor if it stands at least a couple of hours before being reheated and served. To thicken, either mash some of the potato pieces and simmer, or make a roux by lightly browning 4 tablespoons flour in 4 tablespoons unsalted butter, beat it into the simmering soup, and cook 10 minutes longer. Adjust seasonings. Serve sprinkled with chopped parsley, passing thick slices of toasted Italian-style bread or German rolls.

The open-air vegetable stalls in Munich's Viktualienmarkt are enclosed with plastic sheets during the winter months.

The table is set, and I have found

the good old German flavor.

You greeted me, my Sauerkraut,

With your most charming savor.

—"Ode to Sauerkraut" by Heinrich Heine

A cheese shop in Palermo's Ballarò market.

The beloved Mercato della Vucciria, a collection of winding alleys, is located in the heart of Palermo. This inviting shop sells local olives, chestnuts, peppers, and olive oil.

Wonderful Ways with White Truffles

In describing feasts where truffles were served for their aphrodisiac properties, the fifteenth-century gastronome and writer Bartolomeo de Sacchi de Piadena, better known as Platina, observed, "If this is done for the sake of procreation it is praiseworthy. But if it is for libidinousness (as the idle and intemperate are wont to do) then it is altogether detestable" (from *The Honest Voluptuary*, 1475, the oldest known cookbook in print).

Although the Langhe hills of Piedmont do produce some black truffles (far more the specialty of Umbria), it is the white ones—really tannish-buff—that are the real prizes. They have a deeper, headier aroma, sometimes described as pubescent, and a flavor that hints of ripe Camembert, cauliflower, and ancient history. Look for truffles that are smooth (to avoid dirt pockets) and firm, and with little mottling and no worm holes. They should not be displayed for long in the open air, but rather enclosed, preferably in the arborio rice of the same region. The rice protects the truffles from air and moisture, and the truffles flavor the rice as a base for risotto. If serving truffles, spring for a handheld truffle shaver so paper-thin slices of this costly ingredient can be dispensed with both economy and finesse.

White truffles are rarely cooked; rather, they are shaved raw and used in a number of dishes that show them to advantage: atop omelets or scrambled eggs; over fettuccine tossed with butter and grated Parmesan; into salads with wild mushrooms such as *òvoli* and chanterelles, or with asparagus and celery; and layered into a buttered gratin dish to be baked under a mantle of fontina, the buttery, semisoft cheese of the same region that naturally carries a hint of truffle flavor. Most luxuriously, the white truffle is also the defining ingredient in Piedmont's classic risotto.

The renowned Mercato del Tartufo is held from October to December in Alba, the Piedmont region's famous center for truffles. Each truffle is displayed and tagged with its staggeringly high price.

One must examine, touch, and sniff an aromatic white truffle in order to determine its quality.

Pescespada Messinese
Swordfish, Messina Style

This dish is also known as *pescespada ghiotta,* named for the piquant tomato sauce flavored with those other Sicilian favorites, capers and olives. Shop for fresh swordfish rather than frozen and look for flesh with a solid white color and a fine grain rather than an open grain, and with no blood spots. It is best if the fishmonger cuts your slices to order.

    For six servings, buy 6 thin slices of swordfish (about 2 pounds). Sprinkle them with coarse salt and let them stand while you prepare the sauce. In a deep, heavy skillet, large enough to hold the fish in a single layer, heat $\frac{1}{2}$ cup olive oil and in it sauté 1 medium diced onion, $\frac{2}{3}$ cup diced celery, and $\frac{1}{2}$ cup chopped parsley until the vegetables are soft but not colored. Stir in 2 cups plain tomato or marinara sauce made without tomato paste and bring to a simmer. Rinse the fish of salt and add it to the pan, gently pushing down and turning to cover it with sauce. Add about 1 cup pitted black Sicilian olives, $\frac{1}{2}$ cup pitted green olives, and 5 or 6 tablespoons rinsed capers. Cover and simmer gently for about 8 minutes, then add 2 peeled and sliced boiled potatoes and cook for a few minutes more, until fish is done and potatoes are hot. Trickle in a little water if sauce is in danger of scorching. Check seasonings, adding a tiny bit of hot red-pepper flakes if you like, or, for a milder finish, black pepper. This is as good at room temperature as it is hot.

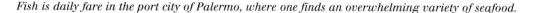

Fish is daily fare in the port city of Palermo, where one finds an overwhelming variety of seafood.

Swordfish and tuna displays are memorable in Palermo. The swordfish begins its day whole, its sword proudly facing the sky; by the end of the day, only the head remains. Sicilian tuna is renowned the world over.

Tonno

Tuna

This beefy, roseate fish is favored throughout Italy. Mostly canned or jarred in pure olive oil, tuna is served as an appetizer with white beans or over crinkly frisé lettuce or arugula, or simmered into a pasta sauce with tomatoes and peas. But the real treat, especially in Sicily, is freshly caught tuna brushed with herbed olive oil and seared on a hot iron or stone griddle. *Ventresca*, the most succulent belly meat, is the costliest cut and hard to come by because it is also preferred by the Japanese, who use this pale, richly fatty portion they call *toro* for sushi and sashimi. Each year Japanese buyers go to Sicily, just as they do to all prime tuna sources in the world, and bid top dollar for the *ventresca* cuts. When buying tuna, try to have it sliced to order from a large piece and avoid any that is blackish, dry, or with an open grain.

A smiling Sicilian vendor.

The butchers of the Ballarò market in Palermo cut and dress veal, goat, lamb, and pork in front of their customers to assure them of freshness.

Agnello al Forno

Roasted Lamb

Baby goat—*capretto*—is often prepared in the same spare and elegant manner as lamb. Buy tender baby lamb or goat, allowing ½ pound lamb per person, or about ¾ pound goat, which tends to be bonier. Italians, especially in the South, prefer roasted meat quite well-done—almost spoon-tender. Rub a 4- to 5-pound well-trimmed leg of lamb (or half-leg) with ½ cup olive oil, salt, pepper, and about 1 teaspoon each chopped rosemary leaves and crushed dried or fresh thyme. If you like garlic, insert a few thin slices around the leg. Place on a rack in an open pan and roast in a preheated 350-degree oven, allowing 25 minutes per pound for meat that is medium to well-done. If you want the meat very well-done, in the Italian style, allow 30 minutes per pound and cover the roasting pan for the last half of the cooking time. In either case, baste several times with pan juices, adding a little water or dry white wine to the pan if the juices evaporate. Slice the lamb thinly and cover with degreased pan juices, into which you have squeezed a little fresh lemon juice. This is especially good with roasted potatoes and cooked artichoke hearts.

Cactus, or Prickly, Pears

(also known as Indian Figs)

Ranging in color from pale green to deep magenta, with yellows, golds, and reds in between, these thorny berry fruits of the cactus plant inspire marzipan look-alikes in Sicily, but look artificial even when real. They are usually eaten out of hand, with devotees ignoring the many seeds. Combined with bananas, pineapple, grapes, and oranges, they are refreshing additions to fruit salads. Liqueurs, a bit of sugar or honey, and citrus juices blend for a suitable dressing. Peeled and puréed, cactus pears can be whipped into cool drinks, alcoholic or not. Ripe cactus pears will yield slightly to hand pressure but should not be mushy, moldy, faded, or withered.

Looking almost artificial, juicy cactus pears are popular all over Sicily.

Opposite: An overflowing vegetable stand early in the day at the Trieste market.

L A T I N

A M E R I C A

Latin America

Among the first foreign visitors to be dazzled by markets in what is today called Latin America were Hernán Cortés and his entourage of Spanish soldiers and prelates, who began their conquest from Cuba in 1519. Bernardino de Sahagún, a Franciscan friar who arrived in 1529, recorded descriptions of the bustling activity and enormous variety in the market of the Aztec

capital, Tenochtitlán, today's Mexico City. In his voluminous *Historia General de las Cosas de Nueva España*, he wrote with awe of Montezuma's direction of that market, with precisely organized separate areas for jewels, gold and silver, feathers, baskets, fabrics and clothing, and especially foods—an early example of modern supermarket merchandising. Sahagún's accounts would serve as well today in describing the enormous and passionate Mercado de la Merced in contemporary Mexico City: the tortilla makers patting corn dough into rounds, baking them on griddles, and selling them plain or filled with stewed meats or beans; the myriad hot chilies; and the rainbows of dried beans, roots, and tropical fruits.

Much the same was true of the Incan markets in Cuzco, observed by the Spanish conqueror Francisco Pizarro upon his arrival in 1533. He and his men were astonished at the chilies as well as the red, white, yellow, purple, and black potatoes that the Incans cooked in every possible way, as do modern-day Peruvians who shop in the markets of Lima, Cuzco, Chincheros, and Pisac.

The Indian legacy is still very much in evidence in the markets of Peru and Guatemala, particularly in the highlands of these countries where the Indian populations predominate. In Pisac, a village located in the Sacred Valley of the Incas high up in the Andes, vendors and the local clientele conduct business in Quechua, the

Previous pages: The market in Pisac, Peru, is known for selling food as well as clothes, crafts, and other goods.

Left: Mexico City's Mercado de la Merced is one of the largest enclosed markets in the world.

The weekly market in the Guatemalan village of Nahualá is held in the main square fronting the church.

Villagers exchange gossip at the market in San Francisco el Alto, Guatemala.

language of their Incan forebears. And in the Guatemalan town of Sololá and the communities surrounding Lake Atitlán, one encounters descendants of the Maya wearing traditional, brilliantly colored garments made of woven textiles whose patterns and styles are unique to each village.

Walking through the lush markets of Central and South America today, one can read the history of conquest and colonization in the food products displayed. To the native provender of Mexico, Peru, Argentina, Colombia, Chile, Bolivia, and Brazil, the Spanish and Portuguese added domesticated food animals such as chickens and pigs (providing lard as a cooking fat and the ubiquitous snack of pork cracklings known as *chicharrónes*), rice, garlic and onions, many types of fruits and vegetables, and spices now deemed essential to the Latin American kitchen. In return, European pantries were enriched with New World staples such as corn, potatoes, tomatoes, peanuts, cashews, chocolate, and coffee, among others.

Added to the mix were African products brought by slaves, most especially to Brazil. Nowhere is this African heritage more evident than in the tropical port city of Salvador, formerly known as Bahia, which, as Brazil's colonial capital, was a center for the slave trade surrounded by sugar plantations. The slaves relied on their native skills in raising such familiar local crops as yams, coconuts, and bananas, and introduced okra, many spices, and the thick yellow-red dendê palm oil still favored in Bahian-style cooking—heavy-going indeed for the gastrointestinal tracts of the uninitiated. The Africans learned to appreciate the nutritious and versatile cassava or manioc root, also known in Latin America as *yuca*, which after processing yields the thickening agent tapioca. This important root forms the basis of the mash known as *farofa*, which is served as an accompaniment to *feijoada*, the savory Brazilian bean-and-meat dish. In certain parts of Latin America, as in the southern United States, African slaves were the cooks, and their flavor-enriching techniques and zesty seasonings ultimately influenced the regional cuisine, not to mention the types of produce and cooking utensils available in markets.

Hungry shoppers in Latin American markets find sustenance provided in *comedores,* essentially snack bars where cheap, informal meals are prepared for immediate consumption or taking home. Today's market cooks are occupational descendants of the sixteenth-century vendors of tortillas and grilled meats that delighted the Spanish in Mexico, and of the purveyors of breakfast foods in the morning fish markets of Bahia in 1925, as described by Jorge Amado in *Gabriela, Clove and Cinnamon:*

> Negro women were selling porridge, corn on the cob, tapioca cakes, and steamed rice with coconut milk. . . . and the fishermen [were] arriving, their baskets filled with snooks and dorados gleaming like silver blades in the morning light.

Now that so many Latin American fruits and vegetables are becoming familiar all over the United States, one might expect them to seem less exotic in markets on native ground. But the ways in which they are displayed, the condiments around them, and, most of all, the spirit and style of the vendors and shoppers inspire romance and excitement, a combination that, like delicate wines, does not travel well.

A Salvadoran boy sells acerola, a tart, cherrylike fruit that is often pressed into juice.

A truck filled with mangoes arrives at the São Joaquim market in Salvador, Brazil.

Featured Markets

Mexico

✳ Mercado de la Merced, Mexico City—One of the world's largest covered food markets, housed in a conglomeration of modern buildings located east of the city's Zócalo center

Guatemala

✳ Chichicastenango—A large market for Indian crafts, textiles, dry goods, and food in this highland town; held Thursdays and Saturdays

✳ San Francisco el Alto—The largest weekly market in the country, attracting vendors and buyers from the surrounding Quezaltenango valley; food, textiles, pottery, and other general merchandise sold in the town's main plaza; livestock market on a plateau above the town; held Fridays

✳ Sololá—A regional market in this colorful Indian town in the vicinity of Lake Atitlán; held Tuesdays and Fridays

✳ Nahualá—A small local market in this highland village; operates Thursdays and Sundays

Peru

✳ Mercado Central, Lima—A large general market occupying a whole city block and spilling over into the surrounding streets

✳ Pisac—A Sunday market in this Andean village north of Cuzco

Brazil

✳ Río de Janeiro—A roving daily market, shown here in the upscale resort area of Ipanema

✳ Mercado São Joaquim, Salvador (Bahia)—A large daily market selling seafood, fruits, and vegetables from waterfront *barracas,* or stalls, in this tropical port

One of the largest and most attractive markets in Guatemala is held in San Francisco el Alto, a town in the Quezaltenango valley.

Hot Chilies

All in the capsicum family, chilies are the fiery cousins of sweet bell peppers, and like them, they become sweeter in flavor as they ripen from green to red. Because of their searing, volatile oils, they must be handled carefully, fresh or dried, the latter usually being the stronger. For the hottest flavor, leave seeds in, otherwise discard. Following are the chilies most prevalent in Latin American markets.

- Cascabel—A firm, cherry-shaped pepper, dries reddish-brown; moderately hot
- Cayenne—A small to medium, long and thin, red or green firecrackerlike pepper; always hot
- Cherry—Green to red and sweet to mild; a round pepper of the sort served pickled in brine
- Chilaca or Pasilla—The first name refers to this long, thin pepper when fresh and dark green, the second to the dried that is smoky black; both moderately hot
- Chilacate—Mexican name for the dried New Mexican (Anaheim, Colorado, and Hatch) chili that is long, green to red, and moderately hot; used for *chiles rellenos* in the American Southwest
- Chipotle—The name for any hot chilies that are smoke-dried
- Habañero—Almost round with a slight point at the bottom, may be green, orange, or red; extremely hot
- Hontanka—A thin, red, shriveled, fiery pepper; native to Japan and much favored in Latin America
- Jalapeño—Green to red with a wide, elongated shape; now being cultivated in mild versions for those who want hot peppers without the heat
- Mirasol or Guajillo—The first name refers to this wide oval pepper when fresh and colored bronze to terra-cotta, the second when it is dried to a reddish-brown hue
- Pimenta de Malagueta or Bird Peppers—Tiny, green to red, and very hot; made into sauces in Brazil to spark *feijoada,* the national dish
- Poblano or Ancho—The first name refers to this wide, fat pepper when fresh and dark green, the second to its reddish-brown dried version; both moderately hot and richly flavored; the poblano used for *chiles rellenos* in Mexico and Guatemala
- Scotch Bonnet—A tiny, lantern-shaped pepper ranging in color from green to orange; incendiary flavor
- Serrano—A small, compact, elongated oval ranging from hot to very hot
- Tabasco—A small, elongated oval ranging in color from yellow to red; very hot

Fresh and dried, mild to stinging hot—a wide variety of chili peppers can be found at markets throughout Mexico and Latin America.

Aztec Tortilla Soup

Crisp tortilla strips add body to this colorful
broth.

    Heat $1/3$ cup light olive or corn oil in a
small skillet and in it sauté 2 minced garlic
cloves, 1 medium chopped onion, and 1 fresh
or canned chopped jalapeño pepper for about
5 minutes, or until onion is soft but not colored.
Add to 2 quarts simmering, well-seasoned, degreased chicken broth along with 2 cups diced,
cooked chicken breast and 2 fresh tomatoes
that have been peeled, seeded, and chopped.
Cook gently for 15 minutes, then add salt and
pepper to taste. While soup cooks, cut 6 corn
tortillas into $1/2$-inch wide strips and fry slowly
in 3 tablespoons olive or corn oil, turning so
the strips become evenly golden brown. Fry
one layer at a time. Drain on paper towel.
Ladle soup into warm bowls and garnish with
tortilla strips, chopped green or red chili peppers, diced avocado, grated Monterey Jack
cheese, and fresh cilantro leaves. Pass lime
wedges and sour cream at the table.

*Opposite: Freshly grilled blue
and yellow corn is a popular
snack all over Mexico.*

An entire aisle of La Merced in Mexico City is devoted to nopales, the succulent cactus paddles that are used a number of ways in Mexican cooking.

Cactus

Nopales, the wide, thin paddles of nopals, or pear-bearing cactus, are delicious when steamed or roasted and made into salads, relish, or candy. With a flavor and viscosity much like okra, they can also be eaten raw. It is obviously tricky to peel off the thorny spines, but devotees think it worthwhile for this nourishing plant, now considered beneficial in treating adult-onset diabetes. In many markets, *nopales* are sold already peeled. The oval, needle-studded fruit of the nopal—known as the prickly, or cactus, pear—is eaten out of hand, pressed into drinks, or cut into fruit salads.

Loading cabbages onto a truck in the Sololá market.

Descendants of the Maya, the women of Sololá dress in traditional woven garments.

Frijoles Negros
Black Beans

A Guatemalan woman sells the basic ingredients for frijoles negros.

Also known as turtle beans, black beans are considered lucky for New Year's Day, especially in Cuba, where they are served with white rice in a dish known as Moors and Christians (*Moros y Cristianos*). Similar basic preparations prevail throughout Latin America. In Brazil, black beans are served with many cuts of fresh and cured beef and pork to become the national dish, *feijoada*. In Mexico and Guatemala they are mashed and simmered in lard with onions, garlic, and tomatoes for refried beans (*frijoles refritos*) to be spooned into tacos and around *huevos rancheros*. These are the most flavorful of dried beans, with an earthy, smoky essence and a velvety texture. Vegetarians can eliminate the ham bone or meat with only a slight loss of flavor.

Most dried beans available in standard markets need very little, if any, presoaking. Untreated beans in ethnic markets and health food stores may, in which case, soak beans overnight in cold water to cover, then drain excess water and cook. Start with 2 cups beans and, before soaking or cooking, wash in several changes of water, picking out shriveled beans and stones that float to the surface. Place beans in a 3- to 4-quart heavy pot with a small piece of ham bone and/or a chunk of smoky ham. Add 6 or 7 cups water, or to cover, and bring to a boil. Skim foam from the surface, reduce to a simmer, and add 2 bay leaves or 1 sprig of epazote (wormseed), 1 medium chopped onion, 1 chopped garlic clove, and 1 or 2 fresh or canned jalapeño or serrano chili peppers. Simmer gently but steadily, partially covered, for about 1 hour. Stir and add water intermittently if the beans are in danger of scorching. Add salt to taste and 2 tablespoons lard or corn oil. Simmer until beans are completely tender but not overblown, about 1½ hours. Mixture should be quite dry when finished, but not scorched; it is helpful to place a heat insulator disk under pot while simmering. Ham meat can be trimmed of fat, chopped, and returned to beans. For a bit of sophistication, stir in a few tablespoonfuls of dark rum. For extra flavor, sauté some garlic, onion, and chopped tomato in a little oil and stir into cooked beans. Serve with steamed white rice.

A farmer leads her pigs to the livestock market in San Francisco el Alto.

Leaving the Nahualá market with a basket of chickens.

On the way to market.

*Every village in Guatemala
has its own distinct and colorful
costume. A young boy wears
the type of broad-brimmed hat
favored by men in Sololá.*

*The vegetable section of the
Chichicastenango market.*

The Peruvian village
of Pisac, located in
the Sacred Valley of
the Incas near Cuzco,
hosts a popular
market every Sunday.
Stalls with blue
awnings fill the main
square.

Two Indian women buy apples at the Pisac market.

In Lima's Mercado Central, shoppers have their pick from a variety of potatoes, a staple of the Peruvian diet.

A tranquil moment at
Salvador's fish market.

Ceviche

Popular in coastal areas throughout Latin America, this dish should be made with scallops or any white-fleshed saltwater fish, or with tuna. Freshwater fish should not be used because it contains parasites that are destroyed only in cooking.

For 6 appetizer portions, buy 2 pounds of sea scallops, halibut, sole, corbina or sea bass, tuna, or swordfish. Cut the fish into strips about ½ inch wide and 2 inches long. Cut large scallops into horizontal slices. Place in a glass or ceramic dish and add ½ cup lime juice, 2 tablespoons lemon juice, and a light sprinkling of salt. Marinate for 3 hours in the refrigerator, turning several times. Drain off the lime juice and dry the fish on paper towel. Return to rinsed, dried dish and add 2 tablespoons finely minced red onion; 3 fresh ripe tomatoes that are peeled, seeded, and chopped; 1 or 2 fresh, seeded and chopped, red or green jalapeños or serrano chilies; a few drops of fresh lime juice; and a thin drizzle of olive oil (optional). Chill 30 minutes more, then serve at room temperature. Other seasonings sometimes added to this dish are orange juice, powdered cumin, and thyme. Serve directly on plates or on lettuce leaves, garnished with cilantro leaves or chopped parsley.

Camarao Baiana

Bahian Shrimp in Coconut Sauce

Canned coconut milk, now widely available in supermarkets, is an acceptable substitute for the fresh in this mellow, rose-pink dish. To serve 6, peel and devein 2 pounds of fresh, large shrimp (about 18 to 20 per pound) and simmer their shells for 10 minutes in $1\frac{1}{2}$ cups water. Discard shells and reserve water. Place shrimp in a glass bowl with $\frac{1}{4}$ cup lime juice, 1 teaspoon salt, $\frac{1}{2}$ teaspoon freshly ground black pepper, and 2 or 3 peeled and crushed garlic cloves. Marinate at room temperature for 20 to 30 minutes.

Heat $\frac{1}{3}$ cup light oil such as corn or peanut in a 10-inch skillet. Gently sauté until soft 1 large, finely minced onion and 4 chopped scallions using the white and tender green portions. Stir in $\frac{3}{4}$ cup crushed canned tomatoes and half of the shrimp water, adding more as needed to prevent scorching. Simmer until smooth and thick, about 8 minutes. Stir in $1\frac{1}{2}$ cups canned coconut milk. Add shrimp and their marinade and simmer gently for about 5 minutes, or until shrimp are done. Adjust seasonings and serve atop steamed white rice.

Freshly caught jumbo shrimp.

127

From an overflowing shop in the São Joaquim market in Salvador one can purchase produce, pepper sauces, and dendê palm oil, which are common ingredients in Brazilian cuisine.

At the Ipanema market, an orderly array of fresh fruits and vegetables is shaded from the sun.

*Tropical fruit juices are pressed to order
in most Brazilian markets.*

Fruit Juices

With the rainbow of tropical fruits available in Latin America, it is no wonder that their sparkling rich juices are so popular. At markets, cafes, and small street stalls one can order, alone or in combination, juices of the pineapple, mango, papaya, banana, orange, lime, lemon, sugarcane, granadilla, acerola, cherimoya or custard apple, cashew apple, and coconut. Widely known for the curved, sweet-flavored, and meaty nut that is its seed, the soft, peachlike cashew apple may be white, yellow, or red, and is valued for its thirst-quenching, tart-sweet juice. Chilled and punctured to admit a straw, the coconut itself is the container for thin, coolly refreshing milk that is much favored on the beaches of Rio de Janeiro.

A stylish vegetable stand at the Ipanema market.

In Brazil, cashew nuts are sold with the colorful "apple" from which they grow. The cashew apple is squeezed to make a refreshing juice. The nut grows inside a thick poisonous shell that is difficult to remove.

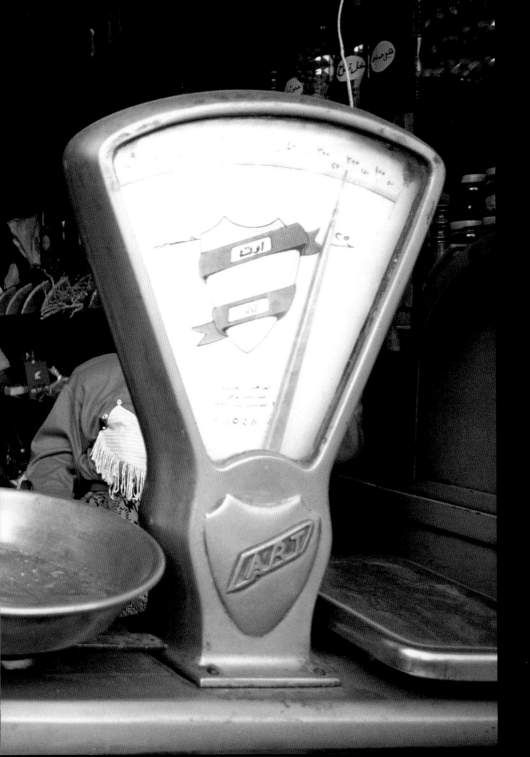

THE
MIDDLE
EAST
AND
NORTH
AFRICA

The Middle East and North Africa

"The Markets of Markets" one could say of the bazaars and souks of the Middle East and North Africa, with their winding, sun-dappled alleys and alluring scents of herbs, spices, cool melons, and grilling meats wafting from stall to stall. Stacks of brass and copper teapots, trays, and coffee grinders shimmer like molten honey in the hot sun, and cones of spices—orange and gold, chrome yellow and terra-cotta, ash green and earthy brown—beguile nostril and eye and set the culinary imagination soaring. Overall there is the clattering noise as the world's supreme merchants hawk wares and bargain with canny customers. Reporting on her visit some fifty years ago to Beirut's Franjeh Souk (Foreigner's Market), the English writer Robin Howe translated vendors' Arabic descriptions of their merchandise to phrases such as "Cucumbers as small and sweet as babies' fingers," and "Apples as red as a bride's blushing cheek," and, a final warning, "Take this price, it is the last chance—after that, farewell."

Nothing is easily sorted out in the Byzantine maze of lands we dub "the Middle East," least of all its boundaries. It is, in fact, easier to define gastronomically than geographically, historically, or philosophically, made up as it is of Christians, Muslims, and Jews. To some the area is still considered "the Orient," as in the Orient Express and the Orientalist painters. Others cut it into parts, placing Greece in Europe rather than in what used to be called the Near East, and identifying separately the Mediterranean lands of Morocco, Algeria, Libya, Tunisia, and Egypt as North African.

Yet all share a common cuisine, albeit with variations, distinguished by myriad uses of rice, beans, eggplant, and okra; skewered meat kabobs; the stuffed vegetables and grape leaves that are dolmas; and staples such as sesame seeds and olives and their oils, yogurt, and piquant white cheeses. Most seductive perhaps is the counterpointed flavor palette of astringent lemon and pungent coriander, warm garlic and cool mint, fiery chilies and sweet onions, the tangy pomegranate and freshly verdant parsley, and the tempering undertones of cumin, cinnamon, and cloves, with a much appreciated gilding of saffron.

Along with their passion for exotically complex spice mixes, Middle Easterners and North Africans share an appetite for unctuous, honeyed sweets of the sort that rewarded harem odalisques in the good old days—suggestively shaped cookies and fritters called Ladies' Thighs, Lovers' Navels, and Sweethearts' Lips. There are also the crisp and flaky phyllo leaves enfolding syrupy nut-filled pastries such as baklava and *bourma*, the supple, sand-colored halvah pressed from sesame seeds, long ropes of pistachio taffy perfumed with rosewater, sugar-dusted jellied

Previous pages: A spice vendor in Cairo's Souq al-Attarin fills plastic bags with turmeric.

Scales of all shapes and sizes occupy an entire little street of the Khan el-Khalili bazaar in Cairo.

candies we call Turkish Delight, and translucent multicolored confections that glisten like stained glass.

With minor variations, this is the menu shared by all countries from Morocco to Egypt, Israel, Yemen, Iran, and Iraq, and even Armenia and Georgia, although few would consider the latter two as Middle Eastern. It is a cuisine now on the cutting edge in the United States, where it is loosely merchandised as Eastern Mediterranean or Med-rim, a tribute not only to its exotic flavors but also to its healthful mix of oils, vegetables, whole grains, and fruits.

Baladi *is a fluffy type of bread that is sold hot and fresh throughout the day in Egypt.*

As in many of the world's markets, superstition and religion are observed in the stalls of the Middle East. In Istanbul's fish markets, one can still sometimes see whole fish adorned with turquoise ceramic beads because that color is said to ward off the evil eye. In Jerusalem and Tel Aviv, many shops display not only photographs of Menachim Schneerson, the late Lubavitcher rebbe believed to be the Moshiach or Messiah, but also a plaque with the hand of Fatima, just in case, and, if the vendor is of Moroccan background, a picture of that country's mystical rabbi-prophet, Baba Sali.

Small wonder that shoppers work up appetites to be satisfied by snacks in small, casual restaurants and at outdoor stands. The bean croquettes, falafel or *tamia,* are as ubiquitous as the small skewers of grilling lamb or the giant vertical spits of beef or lamb that are known as *donner* (ever-turning) kabobs in Turkey, or gyros in Greece, or *chawarma* in Lebanon and Syria. In the gently radiant sunlight filtered through the canopies of Marrakech's souks, one can chew on nougat candy and then find a seller of lemon water to slake the thirst.

Within the fragrant din of Cairo's labyrinthine Khan el-Khalili bazaar are pancake houses (*fatareeny*) baking *fatir,* a flaky Egyptian pizza that is twirled theatrically before being filled with eggs, meat, and cheese, or nuts and cinnamon. And since 1773, shoppers, tourists, and students alike have revived themselves at the bohemian, mirrored Cafe Fishawi, where mint tea, cardamom-scented coffee, and *harkaday,* a chilled red brew of hibiscus petals, are served. The more adventurous try puffing on rented narghiles, the hubbly-bubbly *sheesha* pipes Egyptian men dream by.

The historic Kentriki Agora, the central covered market in Athens, was built in 1879. At its center is a vast assortment of seafood vendors.

No cars are permitted on the Greek island of Hydra, so mules are called into duty.

Featured Markets

Egypt

* Khan el-Khalili, Cairo—A sprawling market selling all sorts of merchandise; includes food vendors and the Souq al-Attarin, with its spice merchants
* Camel market, Bir Eish—A weekly market frequented by Egyptians and Sudanese; until recently, located in the Cairo suburb of Imbaba

Greece

* Kentriki Agora, Athens—The central market located in a traditional market building (c. 1879)
* Hydra—The port market on this mountainous island, one of the Saronic Islands

Israel

* Carmel Market (Shuk HaCarmel), Tel Aviv—The city's largest food market
* Arab Bazaar, Jerusalem—Alleys (some enclosed) of food vendors in small, open-fronted shops, located just behind the Damascus Gate of the Old City and running all the way to the Church of the Holy Sepulchre

Morocco

* Casablanca Fish Market—An intense, colorful harbor market with fish sold directly from boats along the piers
* Marrakech souks—Food merchants in the teeming, noisy, coolly shaded alleys around the operatic square of Djemaa el-Fna

The harbor at Casablanca.

Spices of Life

Nothing is more evocative of Middle Eastern markets than their alluring aromas of spices that beckon one down the sun-dappled alleys of souks. Displayed in burlap sacks, in boxes, or in cone-shaped peaks rising from barrels, their rainbow of gold, red, brass, earth brown, ash green, and terra-cotta suggests their flavors. Following are some of the classic mixes and pastes that inform the cooking of these countries.

❋ Baharat—Iraqi mix of nutmeg, black pepper, coriander, cumin, cloves, cinnamon, cardamom, paprika, and chili

❋ Dukkah—An Egyptian spice blend of nuts, seeds, and cumin

❋ Fenugreek—A yellowish-bronze seed with a warm, bitter flavor prized in spice and curry mixes

❋ Harissa—Spicy North African paste based on red chilies with oil, garlic, cumin, and coriander seeds

❋ Hilbeh—Yemen's fiery relish with antiquely musty fenugreek seeds, cardamom, coriander, and chilies

❋ Hyssop—A biblical herb (and an endangered species) that suggests wild oregano with overtones of sage

❋ Khawayge—Yemenite blend of cardamom, coriander, black pepper, turmeric, and salt for soups, salads, stews, and even coffee

❋ Mastic—A Greek aromatic gum with a mild licorice flavor used in the Middle East for couscous, as well as holiday breads and cakes

❋ Sumac—A pungent, tangy berry that is dried and powdered

❋ Za'tar—Earthy sumac, thyme, hyssop, and toasted ground sesame seeds sprinkled on salads or baked atop lightly oiled pita bread

❋ Zhoug—Pestolike Yemenite sauce of garlic, hot and sweet chilies, coriander, parsley, and fenugreek; either red or green, depending on the chilies used

Shops in Cairo's Souq al-Attarin display a colorful array of spices. Every spice shop in the bazaar makes its own special mixture, in some cases blending over thirty different ingredients.

Two of the most popular sweets in the Middle East are baklava and kounafa. *The hat maker in the background fashions a tarboosh, the traditional Egyptian head covering.*

A minaret looms over a vegetable stand in an open alley of Cairo's old city.

Djemaa el-Fna is the busy hub of Marrakech, where dancers, musicians, and fortune-tellers entertain crowds and a lively marketplace flourishes. This vendor sells, among other items, dried herbs, aphrodisiacs, snakeskin, and a live iguana.

Opposite: Olives and their oil are brought to the Haifa market from the Arab villages in the Galilee region.

In the Old City, behind the Damascus Gate, is Jerusalem's Arab bazaar. Centuries old, the market is made up of enclosed streets and alleys, many covered with arched roofs.

Meze

Assorted Appetizers

Although often prepared at home, the salads, spreads, meats, and fish that make up the dazzling appetizer array known as meze are now often purchased in markets. Such delicatessens display a kaleidoscopic selection of almost a dozen eggplant combinations, ivory-colored sesame tahini, yogurt and hummus (chickpea) dips, stuffed grape leaves, diced feta cheese, the parsley and bulgur salad that is tabbouleh, ground meats fried, baked, or raw in various forms of kibbeh, jewel-toned olives, pickles, grated raw vegetables, and more.

If meze are served directly before a meal, five or six suffice. But if served with drinks in the late afternoon or evening, in the manner of tapas, it is possible to have twenty-five to forty small dishes on the table. Choices might include raw lamb's liver, boiled sheeps' feet, tiny kabobs of lamb, or offal such as spinal cord, spleen, liver, heart, and turkey testicles.

In the hospitable lands of the Middle East, the method of serving meze is telling, as they are dipped into or picked up with torn fragments of pita bread and always from communal bowls, a social icebreaker that implies sharing and trust (that you will not be poisoned). It also means the group must sit fairly close together, traditionally circling low silver, brass, or copper tray tables that are round and, therefore, without the honorific head position. If alcohol is not prohibited (as it is to Muslims), the standard drink with meze is milky, licorice-flavored ouzo (Greece), raki (Turkey), or arrack (Middle East), poured over ice and mixed with water.

Olives

The whole Mediterranean—the sculptures, the palms, the gold beads,

the bearded heroes, the wine, the ideas, the ships. the moonlight,

the winged gorgons, the bronze men, the philosophers—all of it seems

to rise in the sour pungent taste of these black olives between the teeth.

A taste older than meat, older than wine. A taste as old as cold water.

—From *Prospero's Cell* by Lawrence Durrell

Samak bi Taheeni

Fish Baked in Tahini Sauce

Looking for the fish with the clearest eye, the firmest flesh, the reddest gills, and the sweetest aroma, shoppers who appreciate freshness also prefer their market catches prepared in the simplest ways: grilled whole, in slices, or in chunks on skewers; or roasted in the oven and glossed only with lemon juice, a few drops of olive oil, and, one of the great favorites, a supple tahini sauce.

For 2 to 4 servings you will need a 2- to 3-pound white-fleshed fish such as red snapper, striped bass, or sea bass. Fish should be gutted, scaled, and left whole. Sprinkle inside and out with a little coarse salt and refrigerate for 2 or 3 hours. Rinse, pat dry, and let stand at room temperature for 20 minutes before cooking.

Coat bottom of a baking pan with a little olive oil and lay fish in it, brushing a little more oil over the top of the fish and into the cavity. You will need about 2 tablespoons oil. Cover pan loosely with aluminum foil and bake in a 400-degree oven for about 20 minutes.

Meanwhile, sauté 1 cup minced onion in 2 tablespoons olive oil until soft but not brown. Beat onion and oil into $1\frac{1}{2}$ cups tahini sauce (below), adding 1 tablespoon lemon juice. Pour sauce over fish. Reduce oven to 350 degrees and continue baking, uncovered, for 10 to 15 minutes, or until fish flakes easily with a fork and absorbs most of the sauce. This can be served hot but is more savory if it cools at room temperature for 1 hour.

Tahini Sauce

In Middle Eastern shops and health-food stores, you will find the sesame paste, tahini. Beat $\frac{2}{3}$ cup of the paste with 3 to 4 tablespoons lemon juice, $\frac{1}{4}$ cup water, $\frac{1}{4}$ teaspoon salt, a pinch of black pepper, 1 crushed garlic clove, a pinch of cumin, and 3 tablespoons sesame or olive oil. The mixture should be the consistency of beaten yogurt. Adjust seasonings and chill until serving time. Garnish with leaves of chopped parsley or coriander (cilantro). Serve as a sauce with falafel and grilled or roasted lamb, chicken, or fish. This makes about 1 cup.

At the Casablanca pier, baskets of fresh fish are unloaded onto pushcarts headed for the market.

*Breakfast in this Egyptian camel market is almost always a
bowl of stewed fava beans (ful). The reddish-brown beans are
simmered into a rich porridge that is garnished with oil,
onions, eggs, hot peppers, and the like. It is said to be breakfast
for a rich man, lunch for a laborer, and dinner for a pauper.*

*Early spring is the season when fresh fava beans are available,
and the streets are filled with pushcarts brimming with them.*

Miloukhia, *a leafy green vegetable, is a dietary staple much prized throughout the Middle East for its flavor and for the okralike viscosity it lends to soups and stews.*

Lulav and Etrog
Palm and Citron

In the holy days of early fall, Sukkoth markets are held in all of Israel's major cities. At these markets religious Jews select their "Four Species"—palm, citron, willow, and myrtle—required during the week of Sukkoth. Here, the quality and purity of an etrog (citron) are examined at the market in Tel Aviv.

The *lulav,* or palm, and the *etrog,* a citron, along with a sheaf of willow and myrtle, make up the "Four Species" that symbolize the earth's fertility and man's worth. These are important features of Sukkoth, or the Feast of Tabernacles, a weeklong Jewish harvest festival celebrated in autumn and now a national, secular holiday in Israel celebrating harvest, much like the American Thanksgiving. During that week, many families have meals outdoors in *sukkas*—arbors or lean-tos decorated with leafy branches and garlands of flowers and fruit.

The large yellow citron, ordinarily used for marmalade and for its peel, which is candied, is extremely expensive at the special Sukkoth markets that precede the holiday. When perfect, an *etrog* can cost as much as $100 in New York. Canny shoppers push their luck and wait until the last possible hour before the holiday begins in hopes of getting close-out prices from vendors who know their *etrogs* will fetch little the next day, much like Christmas trees on December 26. To safeguard this pricey citrus fruit, many carry it to synagogue in exquisite velvet-lined silver cases shaped like the fruit itself.

When choosing an *etrog,* the careful shopper looks for a bright yellow skin with no blemishes or traces of green or brown, the purest oval shape, and a straight knob extending from the blossom end. When in doubt about a citron's worthiness, the most observant Jew takes it to a rabbi for approval.

A stall in Tel Aviv's Carmel market offers pasta, nuts, and grains,
although the sign on the wall reads "coal."

A shop for nuts and sweets in Jerusalem's Arab bazaar.

Sesame Seeds

Aladdin's "Open sesame" takes on new meaning in the markets of the Middle East, where those tiny, sweet, and earthy seeds adorn breads, garnish salads, give forth a fine and healthful oil, and are ground into paste for sauces such as tahini or for the legendary confection that is halvah. Hardened into bars with sugar and honey, they become another delectable confection. Careful shoppers sniff and bite into a few of the seeds to be sure they are not rancid. Other seeds such as sunflower and pumpkin, and nuts such as almonds, peanuts, and pistachios are favorite nibbling snacks at markets, in the streets, and at sporting events.

The Palestinian town of Jericho is an aromatic oasis filled with date palms, bougainvillea, and tropical fruits.

Spiced Date-and-Nut Spread

One of the world's oldest crops—and an essential fruit for a true Paradise in the Old Testament—dates were highly prized by desert travelers because of their high water content and sugar, helpful in alleviating thirst and providing energy. Groves of graceful date palms with their hanging bunches of green-gold fruit grace the landscapes of most Middle Eastern countries and are among the more romantic displays in markets.

Although Sephardic Jews serve a sweet and fragrant mixture of dates and nuts at Passover as the ritual of Haroset, in which the spread represents the mortar used to build the Temple of Solomon, it is also a popular type of dessert throughout the Middle East. Ingredients vary according to region and the individual cook. It is delicious spread on hot muffins or as a conserve eaten in tiny spoonfuls along with hot tea.

If you would like to include dried figs, soak ½ cup cut-up figs in ¼ cup hot red wine for 15 to 20 minutes, or until soft enough to grind, and reserve leftover wine. Remove pits from 2½ cups dates if you use figs, or 3 cups dates if you do not. Combine in the bowl of a food processor or run through the coarse blade of a food grinder along with ⅓ cup dark raisins, ⅓ cup walnuts, ⅓ cup blanched almonds, 2 tablespoons red wine, ¼ teaspoon cinnamon, a tiny pinch each of cloves and powdered ginger, and, for a lively note, a tiny pinch of ground black pepper. Grind or process to a chunky paste, adding a little wine if necessary and adjusting spices to taste. Pack mixture into a crock, cover, and chill for 24 hours before serving. It will keep for many weeks. Let the mixture warm to room temperature for 15 minutes so it is spreadable. This will make about 3½ cups.

Roasted peanuts, sold in small paper cones, are a popular snack at the markets in Cairo.

A woman sells strawberries along a street in Cairo's Khan el-Khalili.

S U B -
·
S A H A R A N

A F R I C A

Sub-Saharan Africa

Dusty, flat-topped stalls, fruits and vegetables arranged in orderly piles on the ground, throngs of people in both Western and traditional African dress—the markets of sub-Saharan Africa have an unmistakable character. Anyone watching the controlled chaos of early morning at the City Market in Nairobi, as trucks arrive to unload their diverse produce, will be surprised two hours later to see the carefully arranged displays of crafts, vegetables, fruits, and flowers in this indoor market. Signs advertising Coca-Cola and Dunlop tires add brightly decorative, if culturally jarring, touches. In sharp contrast are the teeming markets of Mombasa and Zanzibar, where vendors sit or squat on the ground beside their basketry bowls of fruits and vegetables, or hawk ears of corn that have been roasting over hot coals. And in contrast to the populous city markets are those in more remote areas, often consisting of three or four vendors who set up wherever a crossroad promises customers.

Depending on the location, today's African markets reveal the foreign influences of colonizers and traders from Europe, India, and various Arab lands, who transplanted many foods from their homelands that are now standard fare in Africa. Among such imports are melons and eggplants from India, strawberries and tomatoes from France, and, from Latin America via Portugal, many roots and tubers.

In the brilliantly colorful market of Tilène in the Senegalese city of Dakar, and in the Ghanaian Kaneshi market of Accra, women wear brightly colored cotton dresses and matching turbans that serve as platforms for the baskets balanced on their heads. Determined but with a certain festive air, they bargain for cherry tomatoes, yams, the small white eggplants called garden eggs, and gigantic brown forest snails that will be roasted over hot coals before being sliced and doused with a sauce of lemon juice, oil, and parsley.

Perhaps the most elemental and rustic-looking produce items throughout Africa are the rough-skinned, earth-brown roots and tubers. Among them are manioc, or cassava (also known as *yuca* or, in a dried, refined form, as tapioca), and yellow and white yams that are drier and tougher than the potatoes we call by that name. Providing a rich supply of minerals, starch, and calories, roots and tubers are vital to the African diet. In countries of West Africa such as Ghana and Nigeria, these starches, as well as rice, are cooked until very soft and then mashed and lightly seasoned before being compressed into balls known as *fufu*, which are eaten with soups and stews as Europeans might eat bread. Yams are considered so

Previous pages: The free-wheeling weekly market in Naivasha, Kenya.

Produce is carefully assembled in Nairobi's City Market, which caters to the city's relatively prosperous residents.

important that they are celebrated at many festivals during the year and are among the foods used in life-cycle rituals, signifying plenty and good fortune.

The stubby, thick, bark-covered manioc root is a transplant to Africa from Brazil and has many uses in the kitchen. It becomes a fine flour for baking and frying, turning crisp or slippery soft depending on the type of cooking, and it can be fermented to make *gari,* a mash that is a standby in Ghana. When buying manioc, canny shoppers look for a solid covering of bark with no cracks or mold. In many African markets, it is common to see vendors slicing off a piece of the root to convince potential buyers that the flesh is solid white, much like coconut meat.

The scent of spices perfumes many African markets. None has a longer or more colorful history than cloves, grown primarily on Zanzibar, the East African island just off the coast of Tanzania. These are considered the world's finest cloves, and the oils of the pungent, dried flower buds, with their sweet and woody aroma, are as highly prized for medicines and perfumes as for flavor. An evergreen native to Indonesia, the clove tree was first planted in Zanzibar in

Roots and tubers are important staples of the African diet.

the early nineteenth century by Arab traders, and flourished in the golden clay soil. Less than fifty years later, Zanzibar and its sister island, Pemba, had become the world's leading sources. Visitors to Zanzibar enjoy spice tours of the island's farms and plantations where they may taste the various spices and herbs.

Other virtually ubiquitous merchandise in African markets are bananas, still clinging in bunches to lengths of their thick tree branches, as well as papayas, pineapples, citrus fruits, and

Narok lies at the entrance to the Masai Mara National Reserve. This flour shop is one of the few permanent shops in its small market.

rambutan; bulging sacks of dried beans that are measured out with tin cans; yards and yards of raw sugarcane; and both traditional woven baskets and modern plastic bowls and buckets in a cheerful palette of bright pink, turquoise, lavender, grass green, and apple red.

African markets vary with economic conditions, and in certain places the widespread poverty is very much in evidence. Perhaps one of the world's most poignant markets is the seaside gathering in Senegal's St. Louis, where women meet fishing boats at dawn to vie for what are mostly trash fish, the only kind available to them as better varieties are sold to higher bidders from abroad.

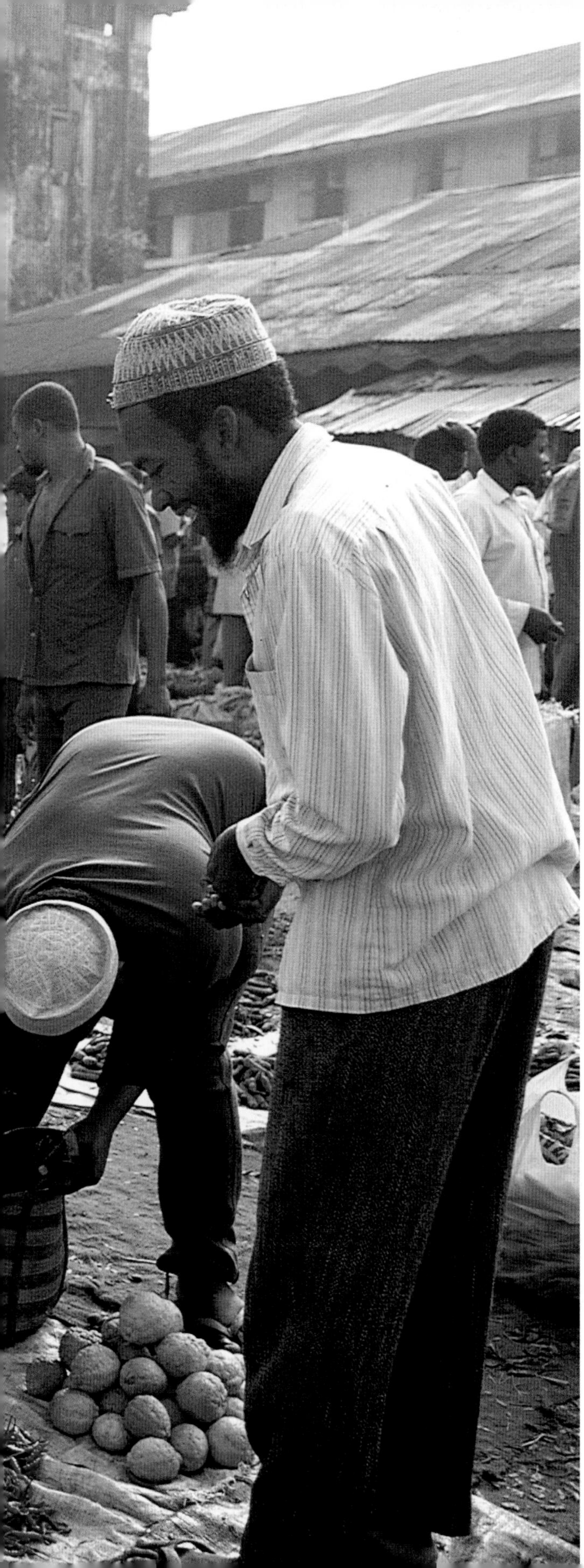

An impromptu market forms in a yard behind Zanzibar's Saidiyeh market.

Featured Markets

Kenya

Nairobi

- City Market—A landmark of the Kenyan capital, an enclosed market with all sorts of souvenirs and food sold in stalls
- Wakulima—The city's main wholesale farmers' market
- Gikomba—The city's center for new and used clothing; also has some food vendors
- City Park—A suburban market on the outskirts of Nairobi
- Kawonlgware—A sprawling market in one of Nairobi's suburbs

Mombasa

- Mckinnon Market—The main market in the center of this large, old port on Africa's east coast
- Kongowea—A wholesale food market in a fishing village just outside Mombasa

Other Locations in Kenya

- Karatina—A market that caters to the Kikuyu people who live in the area of Mount Kenya
- Narok—A small market near the entrance to the Masai Mara National Reserve

Tanzania

Zanzibar

- Saidiyeh Market—A wholesale and retail market for meat, fish, fruits, and vegetables in the capital on the island of Zanzibar
- Fish Market—A sunrise auction on the Zanzibar pier

Oblivious to the tropical rain, a woman picks out the best potatoes in the Kongowea wholesale market just outside Mombasa.

Beans

With limited land for farming and a dire need for quality protein in many African countries, beans are cultivated as dietary staples to be served with corn or other grains as complete protein. Bean dishes vary throughout Africa. Ethiopians serve a salad of lentils spiked with green chilies and, during Lent, fish-shaped crackers made of chickpea flour that are dipped into a fiery red chili relish. In Tanzania and Kenya, red beans and chickpeas are aromatically spiced and simmered with grated coconut or coconut milk. Red beans are also essential in the Kenyan mixed vegetable stew known as *githeri* (see recipe on page 170).

Longtime favorites in African markets are bean cakes, something like the fried croquettes we know as falafel, although made of a smoother mash. That mash can be mixed to the buyer's taste with the additions of shrimp or crayfish, sweet or hot peppers, and spices before being formed and deep-fried in peanut or palm oil until brown and crunchy. The beans used for such cakes are those found in African markets today: brown favas, white broad beans, black-eyed peas, yellow split peas, red kidney beans, buff-colored chickpeas, and tiny red, green, or brown lentils.

A variety of dried beans for sale in Zanzibar.

Vendors of dried beans have their own section at the edge of Nairobi's vast Gikomba market. Each sack is topped with a tin can that serves as a measuring device.

Opposite: The wholesale vendors of Zanzibar's Saidiyeh market.

Githeri

The ingredients in this hearty Kenyan vegetable stew vary with the cook and the season, but the most distinctive are dried red beans, carrots, tomato, onion, kale or cabbage, and dried or fresh corn kernels. Fresh corn makes a light, delicate stew, but the dried produces a more sustaining winter dish. Vegetable oil is a lighter substitute for the authentic but heavy palm oil. Beef is often added.

Soak 1 cup dried red kidney beans or chickpeas in water to cover overnight, and, in a separate bowl, soak 1 cup dried corn kernels, unless you use the fresh. Simmer beans and corn together in salted water to cover for 1 hour, then drain. In a heavy 3-quart dutch oven heat 3 tablespoons light vegetable oil. If using beef, brown 1 pound cubed, lean chuck. In the same pot, sauté 1 large chopped red onion and 1 chopped garlic clove, along with 1 teaspoon dried thyme leaves or 2 teaspoons fresh, and 1 small crumbled bay leaf. When onion is soft but not yet colored, stir in 3 fresh or canned tomatoes that have been skinned and seeded, along with their juice, 2 large sliced carrots, and 1 pound of coarsely chopped kale or green cabbage. Cover and braise gently for 5 minutes. Add beans, dried corn, and about 3 cups meat or chicken broth, or water (for vegetarians). Liquid should be just below the level of the solids. Simmer gently, partially covered, for about 1 hour, stirring occasionally. Add salt and black pepper to taste and stock if mixture becomes dry. If you like, add 2 medium-size peeled and cubed potatoes for the last 20 minutes of cooking time. Instead of dried corn, add 2 cups fresh corn kernels for the last 10 minutes of cooking time. If liquid is too thin, thicken with a little tomato paste. Other seasonings that might be used are pinches of crushed, dried chili pepper, turmeric, cumin, coriander seeds, and cinnamon, in any combination. Serve with steamed white rice. About 6 servings.

The weekly Kawonglware market is located in a suburb of Nairobi.

A group of Kikuyu women pass a chicken vendor at the Karatina market.

Chicken and Peanut Soup

Peanuts and chicken, virtually ubiquitous in markets throughout Africa, are combined in this seductive soup. Peanut butter, whether prepared or homemade, should be unsweetened. To the East African version of this dish, West Africans might also add peeled, cubed sweet potatoes, chopped cabbage, and sliced okra.

Cut a 3-pound chicken into 8 pieces and brown slowly in a skillet with 2 or 3 tablespoons peanut or other light vegetable oil. Place browned chicken in a soup pot. Add to the skillet and sauté until golden 1 chopped medium onion, 1 diced large carrot, and 1 minced garlic clove. Transfer to the soup pot and add 3 chopped fresh or canned tomatoes with their juice, 2 thin slices peeled fresh ginger, 1 small hot red chili pepper, 2 teaspoons salt, and 8 to 10 lightly crushed black peppercorns. Cover the chicken with about 8 cups water or chicken broth. Simmer gently but steadily, partially covered, for about 45 minutes until chicken is completely tender, replenishing water as needed. Remove the chicken and trim the meat from the skin and bones, pulling or cutting the meat into spoon-size pieces. Strain the soup and return it to the rinsed pot with the chicken meat. With a wire whisk, beat 1 cup unsweetened peanut butter and 2 tablespoons tomato paste into the soup until smoothly blended. Simmer for 10 minutes and adjust seasonings, thickening with more peanut butter if necessary. Top each serving with roasted, chopped peanuts. Yields 6 to 8 servings.

Opposite: A Masai man stops at the Narok market to buy potatoes.

*A rainbow of spices enlivens the city market in Mombasa,
which has large Indian and Arabic communities.*

Ginger Beer

Shoppers sniff for astringent freshness as they pick carefully over earthy, gnarled gingerroots, avoiding those that are too dry and woody with age, split, or dusty with mold. This refreshing ginger beer, once popular in the Creole kitchens of Louisiana, was a legacy of African slaves and is the ancestor of ginger ale. It is sometimes fermented with yeast and cream of tartar, or, more mildly, only with sugar or honey. Freshly pressed pineapple, mango, guava, orange, or papaya juice can also be added.

With a vegetable parer, peel ½ pound fresh ginger. Slice, and then pound the ginger with a mortar and pestle or purée it in a food processor, adding just enough water to make the processing possible. Place ginger in a heatproof glass or ceramic bowl. Add 2 quarts boiling water, 1 cup sugar or honey, 6 or 8 cloves, 1 stick of cinnamon, and ½ cup lime or lemon juice with 1 teaspoon grated peel. Cover loosely and keep in a warm place for about 4 hours. Skim off foam, if any. Add 2 quarts cold water, and adjust flavor with sugar or honey and citrus juice. Strain into clean bottles. Cap tightly and store in the refrigerator. This may be served as soon as it is chilled, but it develops more character if it ferments for a week. It will keep for about 2 weeks. Serve over ice as is, or dilute to taste with water or fruit juice, and/or a dash of rum. About 4 quarts.

A truck loaded with sugarcane arrives at Wakulima, Nairobi's central wholesale market.

Double-decker buses ply Zanzibar's Saidiyeh market; the passengers take the lower deck, and their purchases go on top. Here, porters unload baskets of oranges.

*A pile of juicy pineapples
at the Karatina market.*

Pick a Perfect Pineapple

Don't bother plucking a leaf from the crown of the pineapple, as this much-touted test of ripeness is virtually useless. What small, trim, bright green leaves do signal is a fresh, unwilted pineapple. Sniff for a sweet but gently acidic aroma, then check for an even gold-to-rose color with very little green, and with "eyes" that are smooth and prominent, not shrunken. The whole fruit should feel heavy for its volume, indicating juiciness, and should be free of blemishes, soft spots, mold, cracks, or any signs of drying or shriveling. A regular shape, varying with the pineapple variety, also indicates quality. Although a pineapple that is somewhat green at the top will ripen, one that is green at the lower half probably will not, because it was picked before sufficient sugar developed. For an elegant dessert, sprinkle chunks or slices of pineapple with a little sugar and a combination of Grand Marnier and kirsch liqueurs, or dark rum. If you like, pineapple can be combined with an equal amount of cut or sliced ripe papaya and/or mango and sauced in the same way.

Left: A roadside stand on the main route to Karatina sells huge green papayas.

Right: Banana-tree branches still laden with fruit are a striking sight at the Kongowea wholesale market.

Papaya

Although we tend to think of papaya as a melon, this sweet, seductively silky fruit is really a large berry, botanically close to the avocado and the mango. A transplant from Latin America to Africa, the papaya is equally delicious when puréed into juice or a salad dressing, served cold as an appetizer or dessert, or steamed and tossed with butter and nutmeg as a squashlike vegetable. Unripe green papaya lends a coolly refreshing texture to salads. It is low in calories and high in vitamin C and potassium. The leathery skin ranges from yellow to green, the silken flesh varies from yellow to rose pink, and the large cavity holds many big round seeds as shiny as black jet. Shoppers judge a ripe papaya by its sunny, yellow-tinged hue and press gently on the skin to see if the flesh yields, much like that of a ripe avocado. Sliced or served in halves, papaya needs no more enhancement than a drizzle of fresh lime juice.

Banana Fritters

Whatever the size and variety, bananas are universally appreciated when they show black speckles indicating ripeness. If green when purchased, bananas should be bought in bunches, as they rarely ripen individually. Bananas meant to be fried or baked should be half-ripe, but used in these fritters, or in breads and puddings, they should be fully ripe.

Select 5 or 6 medium-size (about 1¼ pounds), fully ripe bananas. Mash with a stainless-steel fork and sprinkle with 2 teaspoons lemon juice. In a mixing bowl, combine ¾ cup flour, ¾ cup cornstarch, 4 tablespoons sugar, ¼ teaspoon each powdered ginger and cinnamon, and ⅛ teaspoon powdered cloves. In a separate bowl, beat 3 extra-large eggs into ¾ cup milk and stir into flour and spice mixture. Mix in bananas.

Heat a 2-inch depth of light vegetable oil in a deep skillet. When hot (375 degrees on a fat thermometer), drop in banana mixture, ¼ cupful at a time, adding only 4 or 5 at a time. Fry about 4 minutes and then turn and fry on the other side until golden brown. Drain on paper towels. Serve as hot as possible, sprinkled with confectioner's sugar or cinnamon sugar. This will make about 24 fritters, enough for 8 to 12 portions.

THE

UNITED

STATES

The United States

In the country where the modern supermarket was invented, the big news is old-time public markets that may be entirely or partly farmers' markets in which independent vendors are the producers of their wares. With their sweet disorder of scents, sights, and sounds, their profusion of flowers, fruits, and vegetables, the din of voices and the allure of sample tastings, these veritable fairs are the antithesis of climate-controlled, antiseptic, and depersonalized supermarkets. Despite traces of soil and a not-too-occasional insect on produce, the confusion of baby carriages and dogs on leashes, the makeshift packaging, and the inconveniences of paying cash and braving the weather, when well-conceived and -operated these markets thrive, indoors and out, even—or, perhaps, especially—within the concrete- and skyscraper-bound confines of large cities. So popular are public markets that a nonprofit organization, Public Market Partners in New York, works continually with communities across the country, advising on the planning and operation of such facilities.

Previous pages: Seattle's Pike Place Market is organized as a long corridor with meat and fish stalls along one side and vegetables on the other.

What farmers' markets provide in a practical way is fresher produce than most retail stores can match, as crops are picked (or fish caught, or pies baked) in the dark, early hours of market mornings or late on the afternoons before. In addition, they offer many so-called heritage or heirloom strains of fruits and vegetables—romantic, old-fashioned lettuces, tomatoes, berries—that are not genetically engineered to have the long shelf life commercial stores demand. There is also much emphasis on the natural and the organic, not only with produce but with poultry and meat, cheeses, farmed fish, breads, honeys, and jams. As lagniappe, prices at these markets are generally lower than at their gourmet counterparts, because middleman profits are eliminated and work is shared by family members.

There is profit too for the community, from jobs created by the market organizers who need service staffs, and from taxes and rent for the city coffers. Most dramatically, such markets have been responsible for turning around depressed inner-city neighborhoods in places such as New York, Detroit, Hartford, and San Francisco, where the Ferry Plaza Market opened as a one-day

Shoppers at the Union Square market in Manhattan can sample homemade jams and marmalades before buying.

A young woman displays locally cultivated mushrooms at the Union Square market.

festival in 1992 and instantly became so prosperous that it is now looking for a larger, permanent site. Such markets bring to underutilized areas a colorful and benign activity that generally invites the opening of cafés and restaurants, bookstores, and the like. Many such markets become meeting places, and there is further human contact as vendors welcome regular customers and dispense advice on cooking the more unusual foods presented for sale.

These markets also afford the urban dweller a vicarious link to nature by offering an accessible garden that changes with the seasons. Rhubarb, young salad greens, and herbs herald spring along with forsythia and dogwood, followed by strawberries and new peas, lilacs and peonies. Midsummer is marked by the appearance of local corn, peppers, and tomatoes along with cosmos, zinnias, and roses. Then on to chrysanthemums and dried autumn leaves as backdrops for wild mushrooms, game, apples, squashes, and pumpkins, until the Christmas evergreens scent the air with pine and stalls display mounds of potatoes, rutabagas, parsnips, pale green to garnet cabbages, and Brussels sprouts clustered on tall stems.

A perfect example of these features at work is the farmers' market that has become a downtown institution four days a week in New York's Union Square. Like twenty-three other markets throughout four of the city's boroughs (Queens being the exception), it falls under the auspices of Greenmarkets, Inc., a management organization that provides premises and services and approves vendors, making sure that all sell merchandise made or grown in New York State, Pennsylvania, or New Jersey. Union Square, a historic meeting place for soapbox orators with leftist leanings, had declined into a derelict park by 1975, when the Greenmarket opened with twelve vendors paying twenty dollars per square foot for rent. It now supports 120 farm families who service twenty thousand customers on a busy Saturday, and, commensurately, rent has jumped to a reported seventy-five dollars per square foot. Set between Greenwich Village and the Flatiron District, home to many young strivers as well as publishers and advertising agencies, the market scene is a lively one. Many stroll through just to look at each other—as well as at New York State apples, Montauk lobsters and bluefish, and local goat cheeses—while sampling handmade pretzels, spiced hot cider, jams, bits of smoked fish, soybean sprouts, and clam chowder.

Marketplace temptations differ according to region, a testament to the country's diversity. Enclosed against the frequent fine-misted rains, Seattle's Pike Place Market, functioning since 1907 although endangered as "a hindrance to progress" several times, is set on a promontory overlooking Puget Sound. Here at least six kinds of Pacific salmon—from the small, slim coho to the giant king—nest on icy beds, their skins gleaming like silver leaf. Salesclerks hurl these fish back and forth football-style, a major attraction for camera-toting tourists. Huge, hard-shell Dungeness crabs turn crimson in steaming vats, and a dozen or so varieties of stone-gray oysters beckon from stalls and seafood bars that serve them on the half-shell. In summer, free-lance foragers bring wild herbs and mushrooms to be offered along with the famed local Delicious apples, huckleberries, and pears. Hungry shoppers can sustain themselves with bacon and eggs, fish and chowders, Danish apple fritters, Asian noodles, Bavarian liverwurst, English scones and crumpets, and Middle Eastern pita sandwiches. Meaty chunks of pink, kippered salmon, hot-smoked over alderwood in the style of the Northwest Indians, is a favorite take-home souvenir for out-of-town visitors. On Saturdays street musicians provide background music by way of guitars, fiddles, flutes, and dulcimers.

In the enormous soaring building that houses the DeKalb Farmers' Market in Decatur, Georgia, half an hour from Atlanta, the whole mix of that city's new immigrant population can be read in the merchandise, with ingredients and condiments to satisfy palates from Nigeria, Ethiopia, India, Germany, Poland, Russia, Southeast Asia, China, the Philippines, Latin America, the Caribbean—and more. Pennsylvania Dutch buttered pretzels, pork scrapple, and homemade ice cream silken with butterfat beguile shoppers at the Reading Terminal Market in Philadelphia, now over one hundred years old. On Saturday mornings at the River Market, set in Kansas City's weekday wholesale produce market, trucks become makeshift shops displaying Midwestern corn and Missouri's sweet Jonathan apples as local stars. At a small Saturday market held in a parking lot in Evanston, Illinois, from late spring to early autumn, fresh green soybeans on leafy branches attest to the population of Japanese students and faculty at nearby Northwestern University, and bouquets of jewel-like prairie grasses flash black, emerald, gold, and amethyst in the sunlight.

Highly prized Chesapeake Bay crabs and shrimp are steamed with the pungent mix of spices Southerners love on the Municipal Fish Wharf, along Maine Avenue in southwest Washington, D.C., a market dating from 1794 when ships sailed in from the Potomac each morning with their catches. The nine shops—really small shacks with open-front selling stalls—are now on anchored barges. Nowhere is there a wider array of fish: inexpensive varieties are purchased by the locals in this economically depressed neighborhood, while prime choices abound for the diplomatic corps. Market clerks report that Eastern Europeans buy freshwater carp and pike, Germans choose rockfish (striped bass), and Greeks cherish silver snapper. Brazilians like the long ribbon fish that look like flat, silvery snakes. For Central Americans it's tilapia, and the Chinese gather lobsters, shrimp, crabs, flounders, and sea bass.

Asked if market workers are served fish lunches, one clerk answered, "No way! We eat fried chicken, chili, spaghetti, and steak. Period!"

Colorfully abundant farmers' markets exist in rural areas as well, and none is more stunning than the Green Dragon Farmers' Market and Auction that is a festive year-round happening every Friday in Ephrata, Pennsylvania. Here in the midst of tidy, glowingly prosperous Mennonite and Amish farms, the market encompasses twenty acres, accommodating four hundred local growers, shopkeepers, and craftspeople, indoors and out. Not only food but all sorts of dry goods, clothing, household wares, and books are offered here.

Along with fruits and vegetables are meats that testify to the German origins of many of today's inhabitants—strings of sausages and darkly smoked cuts—not to mention hard-boiled eggs pickled red with beet juice, gleaming in big glass jars. Dressed in dark skirts and shirts and wearing neat white organdy caps, women sell the myriad pies they bake. This is, indeed, pie country, where one finds varieties named Love, Sunday, Monday, Wet Bottom, Snitz (dried apples), and the favorite, Shoo-fly, filled with golden-brown, spiced molasses and topped with crumbs. It is sold by the slice at stands and in market cafeterias, where other snacks include Philadelphia cheese steaks, hot dogs, and, especially at outdoor stands, funnel cakes made by pouring batter through funnels into frying fat. The emerging pinwheel of crisp squiggles is then sprinkled with confectioners' sugar and eaten hot.

A centerpiece of activity is the feed auction. Held in a large parking lot that is encircled by trucks piled high with bales of hay, clover, alfalfa, and grass, the market attracts taciturn, weathered farmers, most of whom wear black vests and pants, white shirts, and wide-brimmed yellow straw hats. Following the auctioneer from one truck to another, they bid on lots, but only after inspecting for unwanted traces of mold or wetness, for a bright yellow-green color, and, with clover, for blossoms that are fresh mauve-pink. Horses, one farmer says, prefer timothy hay, while his cattle have a taste for grass, clover, and alfalfa.

Like so many other markets, the Green Dragon is a magnet for tourists, which is somewhat of a mixed blessing. Better to have a solidly reliable local clientele, but here vendors worry about competition from food-chain megastores. And as welcome as tourist traffic is, unbridled success can lead to failure. Frustrated that they cannot partake of market activity by buying perishables, tourists look for things to take home as gifts. Therefore, to reap an even handsomer profit than can be realized from food, market managements make room for crafts—macramé, sweaters, kitschy wall hangings, shearling skins and yarns, and nonperishables such as jams, candies, and dried herbs. Tourists then may create even more crowded conditions, driving local shoppers away. The Pike Place Market is also threatened by such activity, the same sort that has discouraged serious food shoppers at the once-excellent Los Angeles farmers' market and made a sham of the French Market in New Orleans, which was established in the eighteenth century and is considered the country's oldest market operating continuously on the same site. (Boston's sprawling Haymarket is a runner-up.) The French Market now devotes only about one-third of its long, coolly shaded length to food.

Lovers of markets can only hope that Alice Waters, the innovative restaurateur in Berkeley, California, is correct when she predicts, "Farmers' markets will be the heroes of the next century. People recognize real food when they taste it. . . ." Or, less optimistically, might we see the co-opting of the farmers' market format by food mass-producers out to defeat the opposition by seeming to join it? Stay tuned.

Only a few miles from Lancaster, the Green Dragon Market attracts the Mennonite and Amish farmers of Pennsylvania Dutch country.

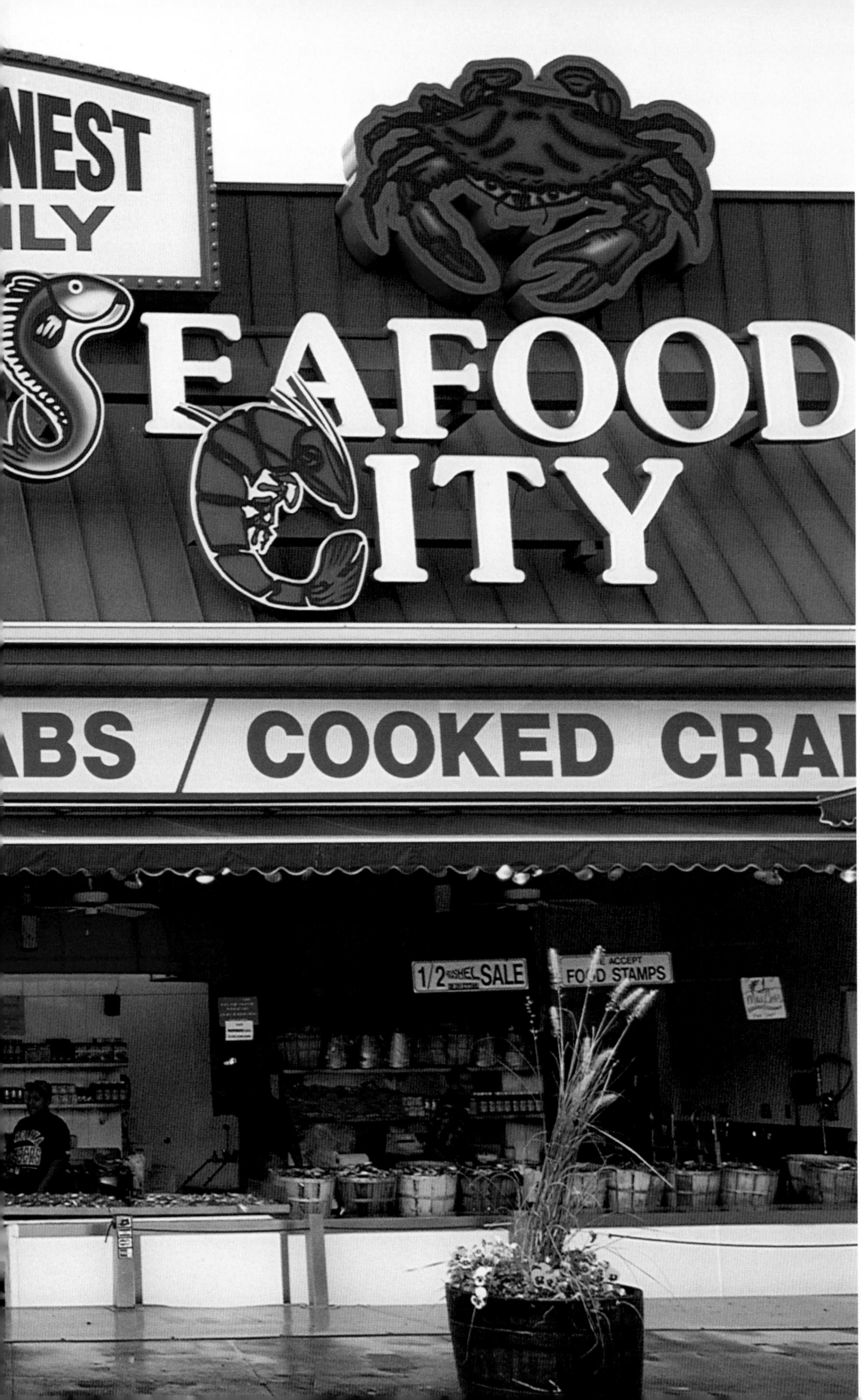

Featured Markets

New York, New York

- Union Square Greenmarket—Operating four days a week, an urban farmers' market that has flourished since 1976

Ephrata, Pennsylvania

- Green Dragon Farmers' Market and Auction—Held every Friday, an enormous Amish and Mennonite market in Pennsylvania Dutch country

Seattle, Washington

- Pike Place Market—A festive daily market in the heart of the city, set on a promontory overlooking Puget Sound

Washington, D.C.

- Maine Avenue Fish Market—Since 1794, a colorful seafood market on the Municipal Fish Wharf

The Maine Avenue fish market in Washington, D.C., on the Potomac River, was originally an assemblage of barges. Today the barges are firmly anchored.

Crabs

Whether raw and alive in their deep gray-blue shells or boiled and bright crimson, crabs are a prominent feature of many coastal fish markets in the United States. Often they are boiled or steamed in giant vats right in the market, and, especially in the South, they are made pungent with the mix of pickling spices known as crab boil.

To many, the prizes are the hard-shelled Chesapeake Bay blue crabs from Maryland and Virginia, with their thumb-size nuggets of firm, pearly backfin meat that has the quintessential, crackling crab flavor. Smaller blue crabs also abound in the Gulf of Mexico, around Texas, Alabama, and Louisiana, but they tend to be mild-flavored and soft in texture due to the warm water.

Among West Coast crabs, the most striking are the gigantic Dungeness, which is close to the celebrated Shanghai crab in texture and flavor, the spiny sea-monster that is the Alaskan king with most of its meat in its long legs, and the smaller Pacific snow crab that has a somewhat elusive flavor. In much of the country, the meat of Dungeness and king crabs is available mainly in frozen form, and, therefore, these varieties have a questionable reputation among serious crab buffs, the meat being somewhat stringy and bland. However, when freshly steamed, both can be silky and richly flavored. Cold, cracked Dungeness crab in mustard sauce is a true gastronomic treat, and very much like the same preparation based on Florida's stone crabs, with their black-tipped claws providing the lushest meat.

When buying fresh, cooked crabmeat, open the container, sniff for a salt-air freshness without any acrid overtones, and look for meat that is firm and shiny. The best crabmeat will not be snowy white, but will show traces of the gray fat and coral roe that add flavor. Washed crabmeat brings a premium price because of its whiteness, but lacks the intense flavor of the unwashed.

At the Washington, D.C., fish market, rubber gloves make handling Chesapeake Bay blue crabs somewhat less hazardous.

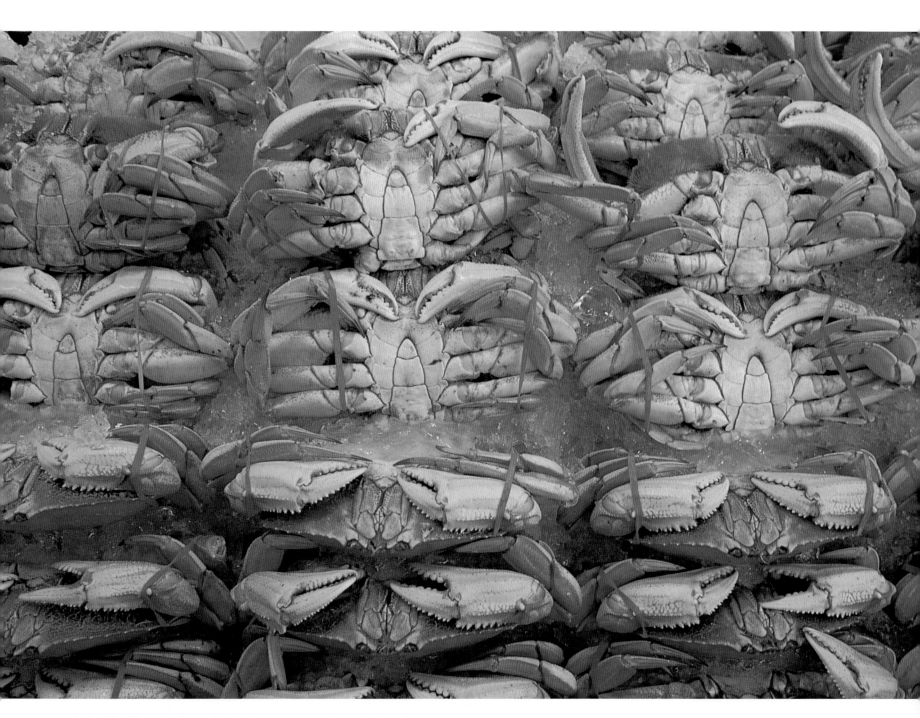

At the Pike Place Market in Seattle, Dungeness crabs are displayed with their claws tied together, for both aesthetic and practical reasons.

If you don't love life, you can't enjoy an oyster.

—Seneca

Oyster Stew

This richly soothing dish is traditional in the United States for both Thanksgiving and New Year's Eve. It is usually available at serious oyster bars, from Puget Sound to Boothbay Harbor. Strong-flavored East Coast oysters from the coldest waters are best for this, those from Louisiana, Florida, and Washington being somewhat milder. Unless you can shuck them yourself, buy freshly shucked oysters and have them packed with their liquid. For 6 servings, buy 36 large or 48 small oysters. Try not to have them opened more than 5 hours before cooking. Store in a glass or ceramic container instead of paper, metal, or plastic.

If oysters seem sandy, pick off sandy bits with your fingers but avoid washing. Remove sediment from the oyster liquid by pouring it through a clean paper coffee filter directly into a saucepan or small skillet; set aside. Prepare stew just before serving. Warm 6 soup bowls. Scald 1 quart half-and-half (milk and cream) and melt in 3 tablespoons unsalted butter. Add oysters to oyster liquid in skillet and simmer 2 or 3 minutes, or just until edges of oysters curl. Add to hot half-and-half with all of the oyster liquid. Season to taste with salt, freshly ground black pepper, a dash of celery salt, and, if you like, a few drops of Worcestershire sauce and/or Tabasco sauce. Ladle into heated soup bowls with 6 to 8 oysters per portion, top with paprika, and serve with seafood biscuits or oyster crackers.

The Washington, D.C., fish market is popular with locals and foreign diplomats alike.

Right: Corn, leeks, and herbs in the Seattle market.

The Union Square market sells a changing assortment of seasonal flowers and produce to nature-starved Manhattanites. Here, sunflowers and fennel.

And those who came were resolved
       to be Englishmen
Gone to the World's end,
       but English every one,
And they ate of the white corn kernels,
       parched in the sun,
And they knew it not,
       But they'd not be English again.

—From "Western Star" by Stephen Vincent Benét

Squashes

Classified as gourd fruits, brilliant squashes (from the Algonquian word *askútasquash*) typify harvest bounty. Whatever the shape and color, when buying squash look for firm, bright, unblemished skin with no irregular shapes or soft spots, and those that feel heavy for their volume, indicating ripeness.

Summer squashes tend to be watery, delicate, quick cooking, and fairly perishable.

* Chayote or Mirliton—Pear-shaped with spring green skin, smooth or hairy
* Cymling or Pattipan—White, flat, and scalloped, with a mild springtime flavor
* Yellow Crookneck—Tapering and straight or curved at the narrow top
* Zucchini or Courgette or Vegetable Marrow—Long or round, with deep green skin that may be mottled, striped, or only faintly marked
* Zucchini Blossoms—Bright yellow, flavorful flowers, particularly good in omelets and risotto or stuffed and fried

Winter squashes are larger and stronger-flavored, require longer cooking, and are good keepers.

* Acorn—Green, yellow, or orange skinned, acorn-shaped
* Butternut or Cushaw—Tannish-gold and bell-shaped, with a thin skin that is edible if not waxed
* Hubbard or Ohio or Mini-blues—A dark green, silvery blue, or deep red-orange giant with knobby skin
* Cheese Pumpkin—Dull orange and drum-shaped, with orange flesh that has a slight cheese flavor
* Pumpkin—Bright, intense orange squash in many sizes, prized as food and Halloween decoration
* Spaghetti—Light yellow and oval, with pale flesh that when baked or boiled pulls out in strings suggesting thin pasta
* Turban—Pinkish yellow or orange and blue-green, with a ridged and drum-shaped bottom and a fluted topknot
* Winter Yellow Crookneck—Heavier than the summer squash and a deeper yellow, with a pebbly skin
* Ornamental Squashes—Small, brightly colored, and often waxed to a gloss

Cold weather brings heaps of winter squash and root vegetables to New York's Union Square market.

Dill Pickles

Kirby cucumbers and fresh dill are a perfect combination.

Opposite: Sniffing fresh basil at the Union Square market.

A culinary trademark in what is known nationally as the New York deli, these juicy, fragrant pickles are of Jewish–Eastern European origin. Use only unwaxed cucumbers for pickling, small and uniform in size, the kirby variety being the best. They should be firm and without signs of withering or soft spots. Fresh dill is essential, and, in late summer, add the sprays of yellow buds of dill gone to seed. Professionally made in large wooden barrels, these pickles can also be cured in glass or ceramic jars or crocks, but not in metal or plastic.

For 20 to 24 pickles you will need a jar or crock of about a 4-quart capacity, with a wide mouth and straight sides so pickles will be held upright. Wash the cucumbers thoroughly, rubbing off sand with your hand or a sponge, but do not break skin. Dry and stand them on end around the sides and on the bottom of the jar so the pickles hold each other erect. Add a second layer if necessary. Lightly crush 7 or 8 whole, unpeeled garlic cloves and add to jar along with 1 teaspoon each black peppercorns, coriander, and mustard seeds, 3 or 4 dried hot chili peppers, 2 bay leaves, and about 12 branches of dill, preferably with seeds. If there are no seeds, add sprigs of fresh dill plus 1 teaspoon dried dill seeds.

Stir ¾ cup uniodized, kosher-type coarse salt into 3 quarts of water. When dissolved, pour into the crock until the pickles are completely covered, allowing the brine to overflow so no air pockets remain. If it does not overflow, slowly pour in cold water until it does.

Stand the jar on a stainproof surface in a cool, shaded corner of the kitchen; do not refrigerate. Have ready a small dish or wooden disk that fits just inside the jar. Place it over the pickles and weigh it down with a clean stone or a glass filled with water, but do not use a metal container. The weight will keep the pickles from floating to the surface and spoiling. Cover loosely with a thin cloth to keep dust out. Every 24 hours, skim off the foam that accumulates and reweight if necessary. The pickles will be half sour in 4 to 5 days, fully sour in about 10 days. When they reach the level of sourness you want, remove the weight, cover the jar tightly, and store in the refrigerator. Pickles will keep for about 1 month if fully covered with brine.

Pumpkin Soup

Cut into chunks about 3 pounds of pumpkin. Scrape out the seeds and the stringy pulp. With a small sharp knife, cut out the flesh and discard the shell. Place the flesh in a 3- to 4-quart soup pot and cover with 6 cups well-flavored, degreased chicken broth and 2 cups water. Add a thinly sliced, medium-size onion, 1 stalk of celery without leaves, 1 sliced carrot, and 1 large, peeled boiling potato. Simmer over moderate heat until pumpkin and all vegetables are completely soft, about 1 hour.

Remove all solids with a slotted spoon and purée in a food processor or with a food mill and return to soup. Season with salt, white pepper, and a bit of grated nutmeg or, for a spicier edge, mace. Over low heat, stir in 4 table-spoons unsalted butter, ²/₃ cup sweet cream, and 1 to 2 tablespoons dry, light sherry. Heat thoroughly but do not boil. Serve at once. Garnish with chopped pistachio nuts or roasted pumpkin seeds. Makes 6 to 8 servings.

*Pumpkins are a traditional
fall staple in this rural
Pennsylvania market.*

Plum Cake

Firm-skinned, red Santa Rosa plums or the small, yellow-fleshed, blue-skinned Italian prunes are best for this late summer and fall cake, especially popular among the Pennsylvania Dutch with their Germanic culinary heritage. Buy plums that have a firm, unblemished skin and no soft spots, and that yield slightly under hand pressure, indicating juiciness.

Wash, dry, and cut in half 2 pounds Santa Rosa or Italian blue plums. Preheat the oven to 350 degrees. Butter and lightly flour the inside of a 9-inch square baking pan. To make the cake dough, sift 2½ cups flour with ⅔ cup sugar, 2 tablespoons baking powder, and a pinch of salt. With a pastry blender, a fork, or your fingertips, rub into flour ½ cup (¼ pound) unsalted butter until the mixture resembles coarse meal. In a separate bowl, combine 2 lightly beaten eggs, ⅔ cup milk, and 1 teaspoon vanilla extract and beat into the flour mixture until you have a wet, thick mass that will drop from a tablespoon. Spread this batter evenly in the prepared pan. Brush the top with melted unsalted butter and arrange the plum halves over it in close, overlapping rows, cut side up. Brush with 2 tablespoons sweet cream and sprinkle with about 1 tablespoon cinnamon and 2 tablespoons sugar. Bake for 30 to 40 minutes, or until the cake is firm and the plums are juicy and light golden brown. Serve warm, cut in squares with vanilla ice cream, or in a deep dish with a little cold sweet cream poured over each portion.

The high quality of these luscious plums and pears at the Green Dragon market justifies the reputation of the Amish as excellent farmers.

Acknowledgments

Travel consultant: Geographical Tours–Neot Hakikar

Commercial support: Fuji Films, Israel; Lufthansa, Israel
Technical information: Nikon, cameras and lenses; Velvia and Kodakchrome EPJ, films; Studio M, Qlab, Israel, laboratory services

Those I owe so much to are, first of all, my family: my wife, Udit, who had a major part in the creation of this book; and my children—Lior, Mika, and Nadav—who managed a normal life while I was away in places too difficult to pronounce and where I never could find the right gifts to bring home.

I want to thank Israel Aharoni, who accompanied me on many travels and whose enthusiasm, optimism, and curiosity has been a constant help for sixteen years; Beth Elon, my agent and friend, without whom this book would still be only an idea; and Mosh Savir, manager of Geographical Tours–Neot Hakikar, for making his staff available to me and for sharing his experience in international travel and other invaluable insights.

To those listed below, I owe a lot. Some contributed with advice, an idea, a scrap of invaluable information; some offered me a bed for the night or a temporary home in a foreign country; some were professionals with whom I worked and who felt a part of this project: Moshe Gilad, Sherry Ansky, Nira Rousso, Leon Botner, Meir Carmon, Moshe Hertzhaim, Jacob Hadar, Ram Oren, Deborah Harris, Modi Ben Shach, Micha Dorfzaun, Ronit Segelman, Ami and Ruth Yaar, Moshe and Irit Stiegman, Yossef and Gali Friedman, Lior and Dick Codor, Leonard (Skip) and Amalia Fink, Dee Dee Meyer, Joan Nathan, Tami Lehman, Karen Lulka, Roni Rubinstein, Liu shi gun, Piero Galvagno, Carlos Raul Morales Catalan, Ibrahim el Samman, Nguyen Hoang Minh, Gita Bhalla, Ktut, Laura, Thomas Burton Hendrickson, Yitzchak Zaroni of Lufthansa, Israel, Antje Flomin of the German National Tourist Board, Israel, PDA Pike Place Market, Yediot Acharonot weekend supplement staff, and the staff of Geographical Tours: Moshe Mena, Muli Shaul, Nir Avieli, Uzi Meiboom, George Zohar, Ruth Chaushu, and Liora Eden.

N.S.

For enabling me to be a part of this book I must thank Beth Elon, who introduced the project, and Paul Gottlieb, who trusted me to write the text and for his patience in waiting for it. Elisa Urbanelli's meticulous editing made sense of it all, for which I am grateful. Carol Robson did a wonderful job designing the book.

I also appreciate the generous help of Joel Patraker, the Special Projects Coordinator of the Union Square Greenmarket in New York, who provided valuable information and access to market vendors. And for especially helpful material on the Green Dragon Farmers' Market in Ephrata, Pennsylvania, I am indebted to Lucinda Hampton of the Pennsylvania Dutch Visitors' Bureau in Lancaster. I also thank Hilary Baum, one of the founders and principals of Public Market Partners, for material on the development of farmers' markets around the country.

M.S.

Bibliography

Amado, Jorge. *Gabriela, Clove and Cinnamon.* 1958. Trans. James L. Taylor and William Grossman. New York: Avon, 1988.

Bugialli, Giuliano. *Foods of Sicily and Sardinia and the Smaller Islands.* New York: Rizzoli, 1996.

Clark, Eleanor. *The Oysters of Locmariaquer.* 1959, 1964. New York: HarperPerennial, 1992.

Covarrubias, Miguel. *Island of Bali.* 1937. New York: Knopf, 1965.

Durrell, Lawrence. *Prospero's Cell.* London: Faber and Faber, 1945.

Girouard, Mark. *Cities & People.* New Haven: Yale University Press, 1985.

Masui, Kazuko, and Tomoko Yamada. *French Cheeses.* London: Dorling Kindersley, 1996.

Platina. *De honesta voluptate (The Honest Voluptuary).* 1475. English trans. and facsimile, St. Louis: Mallinckrodt Chemical Works, 1967.

Polo, Marco. *The Travels of Marco Polo.* Ed. Manuel Kamroff. New York: Modern Library, 1953.

Wells, Patricia. *The Food Lovers' Guide to Paris.* New York: Workman, 1993.

Zola, Emile. *The Belly of Paris.* 1873. Trans. Ernest Alfred Vizetelly. Los Angeles: Sun & Moon Press, 1996.